HOW MUCH IS ENOUGH?

Bringing therapy to an end either too early or prolonging it can be equally counter-productive. *How Much is Enough?* explores the reasons for such unsatisfactory endings and offers advice on avoiding them and achieving a timely conclusion to the therapy.

Using vivid examples and practical guidelines, Lesley Murdin examines the theoretical, technical and ethical aspects of endings. She emphasises that it is not only the patient who needs to change if one is to achieve a satisfactory outcome. The therapist must discover the changes in him/herself which are needed to enable an ending in psychotherapy.

How Much is Enough? is a unique contribution to therapeutic literature, and will prove invaluable to students and professionals alike.

Lesley Murdin is Chair of the Training Committee and Deputy Head of Training at the Westminster Pastoral Foundation, and Chair of the Psychoanalytic Section of UKCP. She is also a psycho-therapist in private practice.

HOW MUCH IS ENOUGH?

Endings in Psychotherapy and Counselling

Lesley Murdin

London and New York

First published 2000
by Routledge
11 New Fetter Lane, London EC4P 4EE

Simultaneously published in the USA and Canada
by Routledge
29 West 35th Street, New York, NY 10001

Routledge is an imprint of the Taylor & Francis Group

© 2000 Lesley Murdin

Typeset in Times by The Florence Group Ltd, Stoodleigh, Devon
Printed and bound in Great Britain by TJ International Ltd, Padstow, Cornwall

British Library Cataloguing in Publication Data
A catalogue record for this book is available from the British Library

Library of Congress Cataloging in Publication Data
Murdin, Lesley.
How much is enough? : endings in psychotherapy and counselling/
Lesley Murdin.
p.   cm.
Includes bibliographical references and index.
1. Psychotherapy–Termination.   I. Title.
RC489. T45M87   2000
616.89′14–DC21   99–30170
CIP

ISBN 0415–18892–X (hbk)
ISBN 0415–18893–8 (pbk)

To Meg: with thanks

CONTENTS

ACKNOWLEDGEMENTS

I should like to thank my husband, Paul Murdin, for advice, support and technical help throughout the seemingly unending process of writing this book.

I should like to thank the following for generous help in reading the manuscript and making invaluable suggestions: Jenny Corrigall, Mary Anne Coate, Meg Errington, Sheila Russell, Fiona Sinclair.

I should also like to thank all my trainees, supervisees and, above all, my patients and clients for all that they have taught me.

The following have kindly granted permission to use extracts from their work: The Estate of Robert Frost for 'Some Say the World Will End in Fire' from *The Complete Poems of Robert Frost* edited by Edward Connery Lathem, published by Jonathan Cape. From 'Fire and Ice' from *The Poetry of Robert Frost*, edited by Edward Connery Lathem, Copyright 1951 by Robert Frost. Copyright 1923, © 1969 by Henry Holt Company, LLC. Reprinted by Permission of Henry Holt and Company, LLC. © Kate Atkinson 1997. Extracted from *Human Croquet* by Kate Atkinson, published by Doubleday, a division of Transworld Publishers Ltd. All rights reserved. Faber and Faber Ltd for an extract of 'As Sweet' from *Serious Concerns* by Wendy Cope.

Every effort has been made to trace copyright holders and obtain permissions. Any omissions brought to our attention will be remedied in future editions.

INTRODUCTION
The problem

Some say the world will end in fire
Some say in ice.
From what I've tasted of desire
I hold with those who favour fire.
                                        (Robert Frost)

The psychoanalytic paradigm has become part of popular culture. It has already lasted for over a hundred years; inevitably there are questions about its survival. Can the body of psychoanalytic theory and technique survive into the twenty-first century or will it be seen as merely a feature of the twentieth century's unsuccessful project for a science of the human mind?

New models of psychotherapy arise and acquire followers and exponents. Integrative models seek to arrive at a positive synthesis that uses the best of the available thinking and practice. There are plenty of new beginnings. Psychoanalysis itself as a discipline gives rise to many varieties of psychoanalytic and psychoanalytically inspired psychotherapy or counselling. All versions of this paradigm share a structure in which some kinds of change are valued and at some point a choice is made to end the work. Psychotherapy is a therapeutic process, not a lifestyle.

Ending by choice rather than necessity implies faith in the future. Psychoanalytic therapy must have the capacity to be flexible and to change, just as it must encompass change and ending for the people who come to therapists. If it is to survive, it will need to be able to tolerate a future that is different from the present or the past. Visions of the future in fiction tend towards the negative. Orwell's *1984* or Huxley's *Brave New World*, for example, have been followed by the films of bleak future worlds: *Star Wars*, *Blade Runner*, *Water World*. Perhaps there is some difficulty in allowing our descendants a better life than we have had. This points immediately to a potential difficulty for therapy. We are all required to work with the finite nature of each individual's therapy. The therapist is continually faced with the need to allow his or her patients to go and, perhaps, to have a better life than he[1] does. In order to do this, the therapist must go through a change and a development with each person he sees. Quite apart from the potential envy of each other's future, both therapist and patient will be faced with loss when ending is to be considered.

Most people come to a therapist, do a reasonable amount of work, get a bit better and leave. There is no great difficulty for either therapist or patient[2] and both are able to come to an agreement on when to end. Unfortunately, this does not always happen. The purpose of this book is to look at the factors that are involved in making an ending and the factors that get in the way of a satisfactory ending. A theory of ending implies a view of what therapy sets out to do. Anyone who offers to work with distress, pain, dysfunctional patterns of thought, feeling and behaviour must have a view about how much can be achieved. The people who come for therapy cannot know beforehand what is possible and, in addition to the basic uncertainty of the therapeutic enterprise, the symptoms themselves may prevent the patient from having a realistic idea of what can be achieved. In any case the therapist might have an entirely different view from that of the patient. This difference in aim is discussed further in Chapter 6.

In this book I shall look at the importance of change in the therapist for the achievement of a satisfactory ending in therapy. Change implies awareness of the way in which aims and values affect the nature of endings as both act and process. The theoretical and technical implications of the kinds of ending that we encounter in psychotherapy and also in training and supervision are also important in arriving at some views of what is necessary or desirable in endings. Endings in therapy can be satisfactory, sometimes scarcely noticed or they can be counter-productive and apparently destructive. Endings across the spectrum will be examined in the light of problems that we encounter in theory and practice and also for what they reveal about individual cases.

We are capable of both seeking and rejecting endings, sometimes both at once. Thinking about the specific character of the ending

---

1   I have used masculine and feminine pronouns indiscriminantly throughout the
     text.
2   The term 'patient' is used throughout because I am mainly although not exclu-
     sively speaking of psychoanalytic work

phase delineates the areas of theory that help to make ending part of a constructive process, rather than merely something that happens to us. Therapists are likely to have a theoretical model which will lead them to be waiting for specific indicators of readiness to end. They may be waiting for something modest and attainable or for an ideal which will never arrive. Therapists are not always good at recognising the right time for a patient to end. Macdonald's study found that the therapist's judgement of whether or not a patient was ready to end bore no significant relation to whether or not the patient reported a satisfactory outcome for the therapy (Macdonald 1992).

The dimensions of the problems of ending are as broad as therapy itself. On the one hand, there are difficulties of different degrees of severity in agreeing to arrive at the act of ending. On the other hand, there are problems inherent in the process itself, created by its nature and by the nature of the men and women who are involved:

> Ms A[3] comes to a therapist because of difficulties in relationships with men. She has been in love with a married man for some time and is consciously aware that he will not leave his wife and three children for her but is unable to let him go. Ms A also has a male friend who has been around for several years but who does not really count. The therapy works by dealing with the way in which she treats the therapist as the person who *is* available. After three years of working, particularly with the way Ms A deals with the therapist's absences, they reach a point where she begins to speak about ending therapy. The first time she mentions it, the therapist interprets it as a way of making him unimportant, like the man friend. This leads to a period of reassessment of the friend (who is present), in contrast to the absent married man (who is desired for his absence). The next time that ending the therapy is mentioned, it is in the context of a much greater ability to accept what is offered in the present. The therapist also has changed enough to be able to agree that this is a good time to stop. The only task then is to decide how long the ending phase should be and to discover what needs to be done before the final session.

---

3   The case material in this book is fictional unless I have indicated otherwise, although it is bound to contain elements related to my experience and memory.

Ms A seems to have had an ordinary, good enough therapy. There was a task which could be agreed by both therapist and patient at the conscious level. She had tried to give up her relationship with a married man. She had not, however, been able to do more than move away physically and give up some of the telephone calls that they were still inclined to make to each other at the beginning of the therapy. She had become very depressed and tearful. She was unable to concentrate on work and had no enjoyment of leisure. In common with everyone else, she wanted to feel better. She described this as being able to be less dependent. Here she and the therapist probably had different views. Ms A was torn by the conflicting desire to have the relationship with the man and also to be free of it and not feel the pain of loss. The therapist might well have understood this conflict but might privately have been thinking that becoming completely independent of other people is not the aim of therapy.

This immediately sets up the tension between goals that is inherent in most therapies and will be discussed further in Chapter 6. An unstated agenda is the need for the aims of both to converge. This means that both will have to change. As the full pain of the confrontation in therapy emerges, Ms A decides that it is time to leave. She has recognised that she chose the married man precisely because he was only ever partly available, leaving her with the option of withdrawing. She has begun to see the possibilities in the man who is available but is taking fright from the possibility of greater commitment to him. The therapist is sure that this ending would not be constructive but would be a flight in the middle of the most difficult and anxious part of therapy. He deduces this from his experience of the course of other therapies and from his own feeling of anxiety and from his knowledge of the processes of therapy.

The conclusion that the therapist reached when ending was first mentioned was that it was not yet time, even though at that point the initial goals had been achieved in that the patient was much less depressed and no longer wept her way through sessions. She had also ended the relationship with the married man so that even though she thought about him at times, she was no longer obsessed by these thoughts. If therapy were merely a matter of achieving goals, this might well have been the agreed ending point. Because therapy is also a matter of process, there were other considerations. The process that had been going on in parallel with the conscious achievement of goals was of course embedded in the relationship with the therapist, where both could acknowledge that more needed to be done.

In some cases more is done in the processes of therapy than is safe. Occasionally, the therapist is tempted to allow a sexual relationship. This causes damage of all sorts because it is always akin to sexual abuse, in that the therapist has power and authority over the patient. Sometimes the result is a long drawn out therapy that saps energy from other aspects of life and leads the patient nowhere. This will be discussed further in subsequent chapters. In the case of Ms A, more useful work was done, in that the therapist did not let her stay where she was, but continued to emphasise the ways in which she minimised his role and she set out to prove to herself that no man was able to supply anything that she lacked. In fact her aim was to prove that she did not lack anything. The therapist refused to accept this version of events, and persisted in seeing a more complex story.

By the time Ms A returned to the idea of leaving she had achieved the ability to see her own attempts to deceive herself and ruefully, but not too triumphantly, point them out to herself and the therapist. At this point, the therapist found her much more likeable and after initially resisting the idea of ending, rather sadly had to acknowledge that there was no reason why they should not. To try to keep her, even if he had that power, would have been to fall into the very trap that she was leaving: to preserve a tantalising, never fulfilled relationship instead of struggling with a living partner.

Mr B is a highly successful accountant. He comes to a therapist because his fiancée is in therapy and has demanded that he too should have therapy. He has never made clear the purpose of the therapy from his point of view, but talks about his difficult relationship with his father who was a famous academic and whose achievement can never be equalled by Mr B however hard he tries. After three months he is saying that he really does not see what use therapy can be to him because he knows he should feel something for the therapist – maybe he should miss her when she goes away on holiday – but in fact he feels nothing. The therapist thinks of this as resistance and hopes that the therapy will enable him to acknowledge his feelings. She does not see the extent to which her own attitude makes him desperate. She does not change.

At the next holiday break he writes to say that he has decided to end the therapy and will not return. The therapist is extremely frustrated by this, feeling that if only he would continue to attend therapy, there could be great changes. She writes and suggests another session to discuss his reasons for leaving but he does not reply.

Mr B's therapy is the kind that most would think of as a failure. He attended for a while, did not seem to be much changed and left suddenly. Because he would not return to discuss his reasons for ending, the therapist was left to process her own emotions and deal with her own loss. She was deprived of the opportunity to change gradually with him and was suddenly wounded both narcissistically in the sense that her view of herself as a competent therapist was dented and also in the sense that she felt bereft. We could all see reasons why there were difficulties. She had approached the work with an agenda of her own. She had desired something even if she had managed to keep it to the level of desiring that the therapy should continue long enough to find a chink in the armour of indifference that Mr B had found it necessary to wear. She could try to console herself by thinking that perhaps he had left because he had discovered that she had made a chink. On the other hand, it was equally possible that he had left out of despair that nothing had taken him sufficiently by surprise to make much of an impression.

These considerations imply that the outcome of a therapy is a matter of technique. To some extent, that is of course the case. It might have been possible for someone more skilled to surprise Mr B out of his fortifications. Such a view is of course based on the theoretical assumption that what is needed is a change at an unconscious level.

Mr B never found his own way to therapy and never acknowledged that he was there for any reason other than the desire of a woman that he should be there. In the first case, he was sent by his fiancée; thereafter he could see his attendance as required by his therapist. It came as no surprise to his therapist that his mother had been very self-centred and had ruled his powerful father by illness and neurosis. He suffered from the memories of his own weakness in the face of his mother's demands and his father's scorn. A satisfactory therapeutic alliance would have been difficult to make in the face of these images. He had learned to hide his own thoughts and wishes from everyone and probably from himself too. His therapist was in the paradoxical position that if she understood him at all he would want to escape from her power, and if she did not she would be useless. Given this situation, the probability of a sudden ending imposed by the patient was high from the outset and might have been avoided only if the therapist had tackled the problem overtly throughout.

Not all therapists would accept such a view. Some forms of psychotherapy would make the assumption that what is needed is a constant feedback of the way in which Mr B is thinking and feeling until he himself sees a need to change and a way to do it. Maybe what he needed was to be convinced that the therapist believed in his ability to work things out for himself. He had a serious difficulty with the way in which he could construct an image of himself as a man. Perhaps he needed more empathy with this aspect of his problem. Yet again, other psychotherapists might have tried to work first with his lack of motivation. He needed to acknowledge that he had a problem before anyone could help him to solve it. Cognitive approaches might have tried to get him to see how he could improve or change his life. Specifically, he could be asked why his fiancée thought he needed therapy and the problem inherent in this area could have been probed and worked through.

Mr B's therapy shows what happens when a therapist approaches a patient with hope and optimism but is not able to find the way in which he needs her to change so that something different can emerge.

Mr C comes to a therapist because he is a writer who is not able to write. He has a job as a journalist for a paper which he despises. He has managed to write a few short stories but is very dissatisfied with them and believes that therapy could help him to unblock. He speaks in a monotone and leaves little space for any interventions. He seems quite content to attend once a week and complain about the way he is treated at work and at home where no one values him according to what he feels that he deserves.

The therapist finds it very easy to sit and say little, although she occasionally galvanises herself into commenting on the way in which he keeps her from being able to join in the events of the session. He successfully prevents this from having any effect by becoming hurt and criticised, leaving the therapist feeling that she has castrated him. The therapy continues with little change. The therapist knows that she needs to change but does not know how. When she mentions ending, he says that therapy is his only hope and without it he will despair.

Mr C's therapy has reached what many therapists would recognise as an impasse. The therapist wishes to end because she cannot believe that she is being any help to Mr C. She has tried every way that she and her supervisor can think of to engage him in discovering his own responsibility for what happens to him. He has not found it tempting to make any move from the paranoid position that he has discovered for himself. Everything is someone else's fault.

When the therapist points this out to him, he accepts what she says as a criticism: 'Yes I know I am hopeless. You have told me before that I ought to get on my feet and pull myself together, and I know that I should, I just don't know how.' The implication is that the therapist should have shown him how and that she is being unreasonably demanding in expecting him to do it for himself. He is firmly stuck in what Kleinians would call the paranoid schizoid position. He pushes all the bad out on to other people or on to parts of himself which he sees as 'other' to what is really him. He cuts himself off from the bad by projecting it out in this way or by saying, 'Yes, yes, you're right' which prevents further thought. His reward is that everything remains the same. There are no risky changes to encounter. The therapy trundles on, week after week, and he feels marginally better each time for having been able to experience the warmth and interest of the therapist's genuine concern for him. The last thing he wants is for it to end.

When the therapist finally ceases agonising over what it might do to him and mentions ending, the effect is devastating. He realises that he will have to move in one direction or another because he cannot stay exactly where he is. His immediate thought is of suicide. That is a mixture of escape for him and punishment of the therapist. An analytic therapist might think of this as a developmental problem. He has all along wanted a mother who would provide all for him and hold him blissfully in her arms. Within the developmental metaphor, one could say that he has not discovered a reason to move forward and in fact is now wishing to return to an even more passive state: death, or, as he might imagine it, a return to the pre-birth state of union and inaction.

The therapist has a serious problem posed to her in this case. If she continues, the therapy could well go on for the rest of Mr C's life. Some of the accounts of therapies recounted in Rosemary Dinnage's book, *One to One* (1988), show a temptation in just this direction. Therapy can become a way of life and the therapist can become a regular adjunct like the hairdresser, although with a

8

greater degree of emotional importance. In fact it is the emotional importance, usually called *dependency* and greatly feared, that is the cause of the difficulty. The therapist is afraid to end the therapy because she thinks Mr C might fall apart, might be worse off than when she is there, and might kill himself. In other words, she acquires some of his belief that she is keeping him alive. This is the belief that he requires of her so that she will allow him to continue in his dysfunctional passivity. In order to be as sure as possible that there is nothing further that she can do, the therapist seeks supervision and consultation from experienced colleagues. She tries various interpretations which make a great deal of sense about his passivity, resistance to change, and his attachment to his current state of mind. Nothing makes any difference, and so for her, the only possibility left is to take the risk of mentioning ending. In order to do so, she has to have achieved a state in which she is confident that it is the best thing for him and that he can manage without her. This may be the only change that is possible for either of them. It may be the one action that will free him. It could go either way. Freud told his patient the Rat man that he could have one more year and this produced satisfactory changes (Freud 1909). Other patients have created uproar and made official complaints against therapists who have, in their view, abandoned them. Very few, to my knowledge, have actually killed themselves.

Ms D is a woman aged 45 who comes to a therapist because she is taking a counselling course. She is a member of an evangelical sect and believes that counselling is the path that God has chosen for her. She is required to have forty sessions of counselling herself as part of the course requirement. The therapist disagrees with this limitation and encourages more involvement with the therapy. Ms D responds with enthusiasm; she comes once, twice, then three times a week. She falls in love with the female therapist and believes that they are meant for each other. She leaves flowers on the therapist's doorstep and telephones her at night and at weekends, asking for more time and extra sessions. After six months, the therapist is unable to stand the onslaught any longer and says that the therapy is not right for Ms D and she will not see her any more. She also suggests that Ms D might like to see a psychiatrist and says that she will write to the GP to explain that the therapy has ceased. Ms D refuses to leave at the end of the session and the therapist has to mention calling the police before she will agree to leave. After a few weeks, Ms D institutes a complaint against the therapist for abandoning the therapy irresponsibly. The therapist receives mysterious telephone calls at odd hours with the number of the caller withheld.

Ms D represents the kind of person for whom the intensity of therapy is difficult and even dangerous. She might manage well enough with cognitive or short-term work that had a very specific goal but even then would be inclined to develop a strong attachment to a therapist who becomes the loved and hated parent figure with power to give or to withhold. When the therapist is as important as this, she may be able to achieve a great deal through suggestion if the patient is compliant. From Freud onwards, therapists have recognised that they are in a unique position to suggest in all sorts of subtle ways that their own belief about what constitutes health or normality is what is right for the patient.

Very often, a therapist feels satisfied if the patient becomes somewhat like him, accepting the same values and acquiring the same thought processes. If this stage is reached, there can often be a peaceful end to the therapy. On the other hand, sooner or later, the therapist will fail to provide what the patient wants. Many patients can accept this and it will be one of their reasons for moving forward. At this moment of disappointment and separateness, however, the disillusionment may be catastrophic and may lead to the kind of rage that makes therapy untenable. Confronted with this fury, many therapists are inclined to be worn down over time or to panic and suddenly withdraw. Instead, of course, the therapist needs to change to a position where she can honestly see that she is contributing to the difficulties. At that point there may be some hope. I shall discuss the kind of difficulty experienced by Ms D further in Chapters 3, 4 and 5.

Each of the above cases represents one point on the spectrum of mutuality and satisfaction that might be achieved in ending therapy. Cases like the first one show the ending of the therapy happening at the time when it stops. In the other cases, the therapy comes to a stop with the act of one of the participants, but there is no process of ending to give it meaning and a place in a lifetime of events so that it can be eventually more or less forgotten. What we do know in such cases is that the therapist is not satisfied. We often do not know what happens for the patient. Each vignette shows that there are crucial points where the therapist's belief, anxiety or wish comes to the forefront, and may precipitate or prevent an ending.

Many complaints received by the professional organisations from patients relate to endings that were too precipitous and were brought about because of the therapist's anxiety and inability or unwillingness to sustain a difficult relationship. On the other hand, persisting with a relationship that has become very negative requires considerable faith in the two people concerned and in the process itself. De Simone is insistent that the therapist does have the responsibility to continue the work no matter what the counter-transference experience may be. She argues that an impasse must be understood in theoretical and technical terms and that dropping the therapy and hence the patient is not acceptable (de Simone 1997: 45). Therapy must continue until the work is done. This is the rule, but, like all rules, it must have exceptions. Sometimes the therapist cannot make the necessary moves in him- or herself and the work becomes destructive. Sometimes external reality intervenes. I shall consider what the occasions for making exceptions might be in the following chapters.

Therapy needs to be lived at full volume and then, when it is ended, it needs to be allowed to fade until only a few moments can be consciously recalled. Obviously therapy needs to come to an end. It costs money. People enter a therapeutic relationship because they want something and sooner or later it may be achieved. Therapy is not intended to be a substitute for life or for relationships outside. Therapists undertake a task in taking someone on for therapy and they need to make the necessary intellectual and emotional adjustments in themselves to enable the patient to reach the end.

References

de Simone, G. (1997) *Ending Analysis*, London: Karnac.
Dinnage, R. (1988) *One to One,* Harmondsworth: Penguin.
Freud, S. (1909) 'Notes upon a case of obsessional neurosis', *SE* 10.
Macdonald, A. (1992) 'Training and outcome in supervised individual psychotherapy', *British Journal of Psychotherapy* 8 (3): 237.

1

WHAT ARE WE WAITING FOR?

Aims and outcomes

Each theoretical model of psychotherapy implies a goal or set of goals and a body of techniques that form a process. In order to be defined as psychotherapy, any procedure must imply that change is possible, even if the change is to return to the original position with renewed conviction or confidence. Whatever the therapist takes to be the purpose of therapy will be a major determinant of his or her willingness to help a patient to end. Even those who decry any kind of normative goals may well be waiting for developments in the patient's ability to philosophise or to be free of conventional thought patterns. Such aims can never be wholly achieved and the therapist will have to settle for less than perfection.

Originally, psychoanalysis was a treatment performed by a doctor on a patient and the cure of symptoms was its aim. It has developed on many fronts but most practitioners today would accept that in spite of the power imbalance between the one who seeks help and the one who is supposed to be an expert, both people must submit to the process although in different ways and to different degrees. Two subjects are involved and both must change if the process is to be valuable.

Freud (1937) says that we are looking for:

- all repression to be lifted
- all the gaps in memory to be filled
- the ego to be strengthened
- the transference to be resolved.

Freud was concerned with memory and the damage that memories can do whether they are consciously held or, worse still, repressed by conscious or unconscious attempts to save oneself from pain.

Clearly, not all memories can be recovered, but Freud's model offers the possibility that at least the most traumatic ones might be. His other criteria are even less absolute. The ego or conscious thinking self is unable reliably to assess its own strength or usefulness. The resolution of transference is often quoted as a goal and will be discussed further in Chapter 2.

To be fair, Freud recognised perfectly well himself that these aims were ideals and could not be achieved in any absolute sense, and that what is achieved is often not permanent. Freud's project was to develop the rational, thinking subject in contact with another. Giving more strength to the conscious, rational processes is re-claiming territory for conscious, civilised use. His image of analytic work was the cultural achievement of draining the Zuyder Zee in Holland. The North Sea is still there and although one can keep it at bay, more water is ready to pour in from the vast ocean of uncon-sciousness beyond to ruin our civilised achievements. Bettelheim (1983) emphasised the cultural aspect of the work in *Freud and Man's Soul*.

Jung also gave a list of possible criteria, some of which are similar to Freud's:

- a more or less complete confession is made
- a new philosophy of life is worked out
- a hard won separation from the childhood psyche is achieved.
    (Fordham 1978)

Separating from the childhood psyche implies the same sort of cultural achievement as Freudian theory. More land is made avail-able for cultivation by separation from the powerful, overwhelming terrors of childhood that continue to lurk just beyond the dikes that we build. Jung adds the idea of discovering religion or perhaps rediscovering the religion of one's childhood. Individuation is perhaps the central concept for Jungian therapy, defined by Samuels (1986: 76) as a person 'becoming himself, whole, and indivisible, distinct from other people or collective psychology'. Like Freud's therapeutic aims, these are statements about progress along a continuum, not an achievement that can be reached.

Lacan challenged the search for wholeness that is implicit in ego strength or individuation, and showed that in his view, Freud's theory of the ego implies that we place too much faith in a func-tion that is supposed to represent rationality and the relationship that we have with reality, but is nevertheless bound to distort and

13

deceive because its task is defensive. It defends against recognition of lack and loss and hence is always against wholeness, since wholeness must include what comes from the unconscious. The best we can do in analytic work will be to track the mysterious passage through chains of signifiers of the elusive and eluding meaning of each individual. We are constituted in and by language, and language is always one step away from the thing itself. We express ourselves in the language that is passed on to us and we are formed by the desires of others.

In this model, therapy works if it can help the individual to find his own desire where it shows through the cracks and the gaps. This desire, like a fish glimpsed and briefly touched, slips through the fingers. While it is held, it may be spoken in what Lacan called 'full speech' instead of our usual 'empty speech'. In his *Ecrits* (Lacan 1977) he said that analysis could end when the patient can speak of himself to the analyst. Before he is able to do this, he will speak of other people's images of him or will not speak directly to the other in the room. He may speak to what he imagines to be the therapist's desire, avoiding what is in his own mind.

Lacan's thinking implies the following goals:

- the unconscious is glimpsed from time to time
- the defensive nature of conscious thought is recognised
- the patient can speak to the therapist about himself.

Relief of symptoms

Many people come to a therapist in order to obtain relief from suffering. Suffering takes many forms, only one of which is apparent in what might be called *symptoms*. Both patient and therapist might wait hopefully for a change in symptoms as described in the presenting problem. The earliest attempts to relieve symptoms psychologically fall under the heading of catharsis and involved the patient in a process of change while the therapist stayed outside it as the doctor or facilitator. The theoretical rationale for the benefits of catharsis is basic Freudian theory. Breuer's work with hysteria discovered the value of 'chimney-sweeping':

> it [the technique] consisted in bringing directly into focus the moment at which the symptoms were formed and in persistently attempting to reproduce the mental processes involved in that situation in order to direct their discharge

along the path of conscious activity. Remembering and
abreaction ... were what was at that time aimed at.

(Freud 1914)

This kind of work was done with the aid of hypnosis and had some
startling and useful results. Nevertheless, its usefulness appeared to
be limited and the cures that were effected were often very short-
lived. It leads to no obvious ending, as the contents of the
unconscious are as broad and deep as the Atlantic.

A small amount of drainage might make a difference, however.
In the early days, the hypnotist gave suggestions that the symptom
should be forbidden to recur. In some cases and up to a point this
worked and still does. If it were sufficient there would be no need
for any of us to look further. Suggestion under hypnosis would be
all that anyone would need. Freud pointed out that the problem was
that this method of treatment might deal well with one symptom
but would leave the cause untreated. Unless there are structural
changes, the patient will not achieve a better resolution of future
conflicts. Hypnotic suggestion does not involve the patient actively:
'Hypnotic treatment leaves the patient inert and unchanged and for
that reason too, equally unable to resist any fresh occasion for falling
ill' (Freud 1917, lecture 28).

There are models of therapy where a great deal is achieved by
working cognitively or behaviourally with one symptom, or we
might say, with the presenting problem (see Chapter 9), where there
is nearly always active involvement of the patient. If the treatment
of one symptom is to be considered sufficient, there must be good
grounds to expect that one piece of changed behaviour will gener-
alise. If the patient is given the opportunity to understand the change,
he may be able to use the understanding in other contexts. Many
therapists would no doubt add that the patient also benefits from
learning that he or she can achieve greater understanding and choice
through the experience of therapy. In this model, the therapy will
usually have an obvious ending when the symptom disappears
or decreases and the therapist will have worked hard but may not
have needed to make such an adjustment in himself, as in long-
term work where the outcome is not predictable to either person
when the work begins.

Freud continued the argument about the nature of the therapeutic
action of therapy by discussing his view that the cause of symptoms
is the repression of forbidden memories and impulses in order to
avoid psychic pain. Because of the extent of the unconscious, the

patient often cannot say enough to complete the cure. Even for minimal improvement, the pain of awareness must be risked and often experienced, or defences will not shift. Given this assumption it is clear that merely expressing the thoughts and feelings available to consciousness will never be enough to effect a considerable or lasting improvement. Other forms of therapy may not accept the hypothesis that the sources of symptoms are unconscious, but most will accept that something is needed from the therapist even if that is not what Freud called the educational function of analytic interpretation:

> This work of overcoming resistance is the essential function of analytic treatment: the patient has to accomplish it and the doctor makes it possible for him with the help of suggestion operating in an *educative* sense.
>
> (Freud 1917, lecture 28)

However much or little they intend to educate the patient, therapists inevitably add something to the work that is done. Pure catharsis with nothing else added is impossible. Saying 'mmm' at a particular point is reinforcing, adding emphasis, showing interest, encouraging, etc. A very minimal kind of listening might be of great value to some people at some times, but it is unlikely to be seen as sufficient by either patient or therapist for most of the problems that people bring. Suggestion is bound to play a part whether covert or overt. Unfortunately, although it may be powerful it is unlikely to be enough if it is overt and specific. For example, a therapist might say after two sessions: 'Now you have brought me your problem and told me your story. You are better, go home.' Suggestion of this sort is often used by the charismatic and in very powerful hands can work for better or worse, but it hardly develops the patient's choice and strength for future new difficulties.

My own conclusion is that relief of symptoms is an honourable goal and cannot be ignored by any therapist. Nevertheless, directly attacking the problem is not enough in the long term. A more complex view of the therapeutic process is needed if there is to be a profound change in an individual. The purpose of therapy must encompass the complexity of the human mind and body. Some writers (e.g. Spence 1982) have argued that the therapist's task is to help the patient to write the autobiography that satisfies him or her by its coherence and the meaning that can be discovered for the person whom the patient is at present. This view of autobiography is clearly distinct from a view that emphasises historical truth.

In this context, what is important and therapeutic is that the story makes sense of a person's memories. A therapist might be comfortable with this role because it does not require much change in him. He is there merely to supply help with the most problematic and apparently senseless memories that a person presents.

Even by adding meaning therefore to the essential purpose, we may still not be addressing the full scope of the therapeutic process which always involves two people who are willing to affect each other and be changed by the impact.

The therapist's management of loss and damage

With some justification, Bowlby (e.g. 1973) and the attachment-based therapists have taken separation and loss as the basis of their theoretical approach. No doubt object relations theorists following Fairbairn (1952) would agree that the premature loss of good or satisfying object relationship is what leads to disturbance and psychic defence. Freud had reached the view that absence is what leads to development: the first thought is the absent breast. So loss has clearly a central position in theoretical structures, and coping with the losses inherent in therapy must require that both patient and therapist learn to accept that loss is both inevitable and can be survived. During the process, there is bound to be resistance from both patient and therapist to facing the painful realities of loss.

Klein and the object relations school provide a view of the aim of analytic work which focuses on damage and repair. The therapist is damaged over and over in fact or in phantasy until both patient and therapist are able to believe in survival. Both partners are guarantors to the other that survival is possible. The therapist hopes that the reliability that he or she provides will be internalised as a sense of goodness in the self so that love and gratitude can prevail at least some of the time and the testing can decrease along with fear and hate and envy. If the therapist's own defences against loss are shaky, he will need the patient to prove to him that loss is temporary and tolerable. The concept of the two positions – paranoid/schizoid and depressive – is a theory of moral development because it implies moving from the unreal world of projection to a greater awareness of the existence of another person. This always implies the possibility of loss as well as concern about its accompanying potential for guilt and repair. On the other hand, facing guilt and the reality of loss is too painful a position to be held indefinitely by either patient or therapist.

Modern Kleinians tend to see value in the cyclical movement between the depressive and paranoid/schizoid positions, with much creative potential resting in the paranoid and schizoid defences. Steiner (1987) has restated this aim in terms of helping the individual to be able to move between these positions with the awareness that nothing lasts for ever. Much will depend on whether the therapist is able to move between the two positions sufficiently to see the patient as a separate whole, rather than as a projection of her own insecurity and damage. If the therapist is still having problems in dealing with loss, the patient becomes the means of denying and objectifying the problem. Another way of stating this view is in terms of what goes on inside the psyche. Kleinians talk in terms of *internal objects* in order to be able to communicate more easily about the two or more sides of an internal conflict. The dominating force in the psyche may cease to be a persecutory and death-dealing avenger, but may become capable of concern and of giving and receiving reparation for the damage that it causes either in reality or in the imagination.

Meltzer points out (1967: 41) that the father enters the child's consciousness as a whole object just as much as the mother at the time of the achievement of the depressive position. When there are two parents who are allowed in the child's mind to love each other, this provides a model for creative and reparative potential to be recognised. Negotiating the Oedipus complex becomes possible. In other words, the patient who has been able to recognise the value of both his father and his mother will be able to allow for his own creative sexual union. When this creativity appears in what the therapist is told, it might well be a marker for the readiness to end therapy. It is not so far from Freud, for whom the achievement of full genital sexuality might be a criterion for ending.

Self psychologists following Kohut (1977) or Kernberg (e.g. 1974) would look at the development of a sense of self through the use of the therapist as *self object*. The therapeutic relationship could be used to echo or amend the early use of the mother or significant other as part of the self for development of a safer structure. Kohut saw the self as a superordinate structure over and above the ego and the id, capable of a sense of wholeness. This sense of self is developed through the use of another person as a *self object*. Clearly the therapist may see himself as a self object for the patient. He may try to help the patient to develop a firmer sense of self, and may enjoy the need that is expressed in this relationship. He may well use the patient as a self object, affirming his own sense of worth and making him feel safer. In this model, the therapy will be able to end when both therapist and patient have achieved a greater degree of self-sufficiency.

The models described so far are based on the structure of the psyche. Change in these structures is brought about by the dialogue with the therapist. What sort of change has taken place will be known primarily through the therapist's experience of the patient, derived from accounts of love and work outside therapy and of course from the experience of being with him or her. Some models, while still implying structural changes, emphasise the parallel to the developmental processes of infancy and childhood. Attachment-based therapies are looking at the blocks in the way of attachment and will see the possibility of ending when, paradoxically, there is a possibility of connection. Differences in theoretical models mean that each therapist is bound to construct a different task for the therapeutic relationship while remaining within the general bound-aries of a model.

Whatever the therapist's purpose, he or she is likely to have to be content with less than might be possible. Gradual failure is built into psychoanalytic theory. The therapist, like the parents, inevitably fails to give the patient all that he or she wants, but this failure should not be catastrophic if it is tempered with the reliability of the setting, the therapist's presence and the steadiness of the technique that is used. Therapists may be well aware of this process and allow movement towards the point at which the patient can manage deprivation and disappointment alone. Therapists are not always equally good at managing their own sense of failure when the patient does not meet the demands of the theoretical model espoused. In addition, the therapist may not be conscious of his or her avoidance of deprivation or disappointment. As long as there is a next session, there is hope of fulfilment. Searles' paper (1965) on the patient as Oedipal love object for the therapist is invaluable, because he is one of the few writers to face the therapist's need and desire for the patient (see Chapter 3).

How much is enough?

The ideal in most models of therapy is that the patient decides how much is enough. We all know that such a position begs many ques-tions. Therapists may not be omnipotent but they have great power for good or ill over many of their patients. They may be waiting for some sort of assurance that the work is well done – that the point of no return has been reached, as Rickman described it (1950). In 1937 Freud raised the question of what the therapist might think is sufficient in 'Analysis terminable and interminable'. Although this was, to some extent, Freud's spiritual testament, nevertheless it does not constitute the last word, and many today would disagree with its central contention. Freud argued that some elements of the psyche are appropriately susceptible to analysis and given a good enough analysis and a good enough patient, the outcome should be an improvement. For Freud, improvement was equated with a reduction of neurotic symptoms. Freud's project is essentially rational and assumes that reason can and should be in control of instinct and impulse. Achieving a reduction of symptoms would also imply greater ego strength in the sense of the ability to perceive and use a shared external reality. An improvement in the ability to share a cultural and social reality might come about through the contact over time with a therapist and would be an aim of many therapists.

Nevertheless, in Freud's view, there is an irreducible something that cannot be analysed. There will be areas that cannot be changed. Once the therapy reaches this hard layer, it may as well stop. He thought that the bedrock of the psyche, the point at which no more could be done for a man or a woman, would be the impossibility of accepting femininity; in other words, penis envy. More recent writers are less likely to accept that there is any universal complex that cannot be resolved or changed, and the outcome of therapy will depend on the existential problems and situations encountered by the individual. The title of Freud's paper suggests that analyses will have in them both terminable and interminable elements and that we can celebrate the necessary acceptance of both, while being prepared to allow an ending that is never perfect or complete.

Perhaps 'how much?' is easier to answer if the work is the kind of counselling that has specific goals related to solving problems in everyday life. If the presenting problem is 'Should I leave my partner?' the work is finished if the decision is made and the step taken. If, however, this presenting problem is seen as posing questions about the need for others or the other as a sign of deficiencies in the sense of self or as a question about gender identity or about paranoia versus reparation, the ending may be much more difficult to recognise. Time-limited work sets the ending from the beginning and enables the process of ending to be extremely valuable, but it obviates the necessity and also the therapeutic value of having to decide about when to end. Instead it demands that the patient and the therapist both have the courage to stick to the contract and end when they have agreed to end (see Chapter 9).

In spite of all the pitfalls, the ending phase of therapy may bring great rewards. In making the decision to end, especially when the theoretical model gives no specific reason to end this month or this year, many of the most difficult and delicate aspects of relating to another human being may need to be negotiated. There will be experiments with leaving at the end of each session, but the choice to leave voluntarily can still feel like a very risky business. The patient will know what partings are like from past experiences and also from the inevitable breaks in therapy for holidays or illness. The final parting will be different if it is allowed to *be* final or at least final as far as the two participants can tell.

Ending is inherently painful if it is fully experienced, but it can bring strength and contentment when it is actually achieved. Much that has belonged to previous partings and deaths can be remembered in order to be set aside. This time a fair amount of sadness may be mixed with the disappointment, and the feelings may be met with a less paranoid response. All of this may involve the therapist, not only as a professional but also in strong personal feelings for what is evoked from his or her own past and also because of what this patient has come to mean. Both people will emerge from the experience changed.

References

Bettelheim, B. (1983) *Freud and Man's Soul*, London: Chatto & Windus.

Bowlby, J. (1973) *Attachment and Loss*, Harmondsworth: Penguin.

de Simone, G. (1997) *Ending Analysis*, London: Karnac.

Fairbairn, M. (1952) *Psychoanalytic Studies of the Personality*, London: Routledge. (Reprinted 1992.)

Fordham, M. (1978) *Technique in Jungian Analysis*, London: Academic Press.

Freud, S. (1914) 'Essay on narcissism', *SE* 14: 67.

Freud, S. (1917) 'General theory of the neuroses', *SE* 17.

Freud, S. (1937) 'Analysis terminable and interminable', *SE* 23.

Kernberg, O. (1974) 'Further contributions to the treatment of narcissistic personalities', *International Journal of Psycho-analysis* 55: 215–240.

Kohut, H. (1977) *The Restoration of the Self*, New York: International Universities Press.

Lacan, J. (1977) *Ecrits*, London: Routledge.

Meltzer, D. (1967) *The Psycho-Analytical Process*, Perthshire, Scotland: Clunie.

Rickmann, J. (1950) 'On the criteria for the termination of analysis', *International Journal of Psycho-analysis* 31.

Samuels, A. (1986) *A Critical Dictionary of Jungian Analysis,* London: Routledge.

Searles, H. (1965) *Collected Papers on Schizophrenia*, London: Maresfield.

Spence, D. (1982) *Narrative Truth and Historical Truth*, New York: Norton.

Steiner, J. (1987) 'The interplay between pathological organisations and the paranoid schizoid and depressive positions', *International Journal of Psycho-analysis* 68: 69.

2

HAPPY ENDINGS

The goal of resolving transference

Only the imagination can embrace the impossible: the golden mountain, the fire breathing dragon, the happy ending.

(Kate Atkinson, *Human Croquet*)

Imagine blindfolding someone and teaching him to make his way across a room filled with tables and chairs. After several attempts, he might be able to pick his way across the room without bumping into anything. If you play a joke on him and remove the furniture, you can watch him pick his way around obstacles that are no longer there. The theory of transference is describing exactly this phenomenon. The patient picks his way around obstacles that no longer exist in the present, but were there at one time in the past or perhaps have been always imaginary.

The analytic theories of psychotherapy postulate, following Freud, that counter-productive manoeuvres to avoid bumping into pain caused by conflict are at the root of neurotic suffering. The way to change these defensive manoeuvres is through re-experiencing with a therapist some of the pain. This will allow a rearrangement of defences and a better way of living with oneself and with others. When therapy is successful, it will be possible to have a satisfactory ending. There are many different ways of stating this basic assumption and humanistic therapies would not place emphasis on defences but would emphasise even more the importance of what happens in the present relationship with the therapist.

We therefore have a situation in which a relationship develops, more or less intentionally, between patient and therapist. Depending on the orientation of the therapist, there will be a greater or lesser degree of mutuality, of interpreting and of restraint. Nevertheless, common to all therapies is the highly significant and emotionally charged relationship that is likely to develop and in some models

23

is encouraged. The problem is then, how and why should such a relationship end and how satisfactory can the ending be? There are two possibilities for models that work with feelings and images transferred from the past on to present experience. Either the old images can be completely dissolved, or a better relationship with the present can be achieved while still preserving some of the emotions and images from the past.

Ernest Gellner, writing a critique of psychoanalytic theory and technique, concludes:

> Modern humans, unlike their peasant ancestors are drilled to expect an astonishingly high standard of logical order. Human work requires it; human education prepares them for it. But when in distress they seek their shepherd, they are instructed to abandon all semantic restraint, and display not only their intimate and shameful secrets, but also the total and deplorable chaos of their mental content, which otherwise they must strive to hide. They must 'free associate'; then it would seem they develop feelings for the person in front of whom they have so abased themselves. The intensity of the feeling so generated appears to confirm the validity both of the theoretical and the specific insights attained in the course of the therapeutic sessions, thus producing that characteristic blend of strong feeling and sense of cognitive and liberating illumination which defines mystical experience.
>
> (In Dryden and Feltham 1992: 52)

If Gellner were right, the therapeutic situation itself might be generating all the effects that we observe in therapy. Frosh, in his response to Gellner (Dryden and Feltham 1992: 53), points out that we can never prove either case. Most therapists would not be unhappy to agree that the therapeutic situation generates powerful emotions particularly towards the therapist. In recent years the emphasis has shifted from the past and the recovery of memories to a much greater reliance on change happening in and through the present relationship with the therapist. The past is seen as corroboration of the truths being discovered in the present.

Therapy undoubtedly generates the specific form of the emotions produced and is responsible for the way in which memories appear and the time at which they appear. Yet this provides an opportunity to engineer a different outcome to situations that have been experienced in essence before. It is both a magnificent opportunity and the source of the greatest dangers in psychotherapy. The question that this chapter will address is how the intense relationship created in therapy can be brought to an end, as to do so deliberately, while inevitable in a professional contract, is contrary to the natural order in any other sort of relationship.

The therapeutic relationship is professional and therefore it is limited. In most psychotherapy there is the payment of a fee. This emphasises the framework of professionalism which keeps limits visible, although some patients welcome the chance to use it as a defence against strong feelings. Psychoanalysts and psychoanalytic psychotherapists tend to address their patients by the title of Mr, Mrs, etc. and to call them *patients* rather than *clients*. This formality does not prevent powerful and passionate emotions from arising, but it does perhaps serve to remind both parties to the work that this is a finite relationship with a limit to it somewhere in time and always a limit to the availability of the therapist. Other formal reminders of limitation are the ends of sessions and the preparations for holidays and breaks when the therapist takes care to make clear that he or she is going away and that although there might be concern for the patient, it will not stop the therapist from leading his or her own life.

There are therefore some inhibitors to prevent the therapeutic relationship from ever developing as an ordinary human relationship. This is just as well, because ordinary human relationships do not have in-built obsolescence or time limits. Friendships may come to a natural end when the common task or connection comes to an end. School or college friends may or may not be kept into later life, and friends made at work may prove not to be as desirable in other contexts. These sorts of limits may arise in therapy too. The task, if it is specific enough, will come to an end. Patients may simply find that they have completed the task sufficiently well, or that they have become bored with a predictable therapist. Therapists might prefer to make efforts, as Lacan suggested, always to be surprising, never to say what is already known, but nevertheless, eventually it may be no bad thing if the therapy is in some sense outgrown, or outworn.

If there is a passionate attachment, a falling in love during the therapy, that may also give a natural shape. Falling in love is much more likely to be followed by disillusionment than is a more moderate valuation of the therapist. Freud wrote his paper 'On transference love' in 1914 to describe the kind of falling in love that happens in therapy. The patient shows us what he or she is like when loving or trying to love and the therapist must accept these feelings without reciprocating them overtly. Since the therapist will not reciprocate, we might expect that ending will come out of despair. The therapist will never respond as the patient wishes and therefore he or she will give up and go elsewhere. This is the Oedipal theory of ending therapy. Just as the child must relinquish the parent whom he can never marry, the patient must relinquish the therapist and move on to other relationships outside. In long-term therapy this may be precisely what happens. On the other hand, there are cases where the patient accepts a kind of stasis with relief, taking just as much as the therapist will give and using it as an excuse not to go any further with anyone else. Some patients never get anywhere near falling in love or loving and leave before there is any risk of that. Some manage to stay without allowing any change and the problem becomes one of finding a way to enable them to end. In short-term or time-limited work, the responsible therapist makes no effort to draw feeling towards himself and the task will not include analysing at first hand the way the patient behaves in intimate relationships. In any case, most patients defend themselves from passionate feelings:

> Ms E is a woman aged 40 who has been seeing a psycho-analytic psychotherapist for some years. She came because her partner seemed very unstable and she was finding it difficult to endure the uncertainty of his next mood or his actions, particularly when he was high. As she talked, she surrounded herself in a flat depression that was difficult to penetrate. She was also very unhappy in her work as a computer operator where her degree was not being used. She had a painfully close connection to her mother but was never able to look her in the eye or to talk to her directly about anything of importance. Everything about her spoke of limitations, either self-imposed or imposed by external circumstances.
>
> Not surprisingly, the therapy became similarly limited. There was much talk about her relationship with her mother who lived alone and exerted a great pull from her cottage in a northern village. Every few weeks Ms E had to visit her mother but was never willing or able to do more than sit in miserable silence, longing to escape. Her father had left when Ms E was 3 years old and her mother had never

remarried. Ms E was aware that she was all her mother had and that she should fill her father's place. This left her with a gender confusion and a refusal as the only alternative to inevitable failure in the role that she had been assigned.

In the therapy she would begin by talking about what had happened during the week but would soon wind down and sit in the miserable and awkward silence that showed the therapist how painful she found it to be with her mother without being able to provide what her mother wanted. The therapist was able to clarify some of this for both of them and Ms E was able to make herself comfortable enough to continue to attend. She was able to gain some comfort over the difficulties with her partner and with the head of the department where she worked. These men, along with the therapist, took on the character of depriving fathers and were punished by her accordingly by being resented and resisted through a passive form of aggression which they did not understand. At the same time, huge demands were made of them that they should understand what she wanted and make clear that they loved her without her having to ask. She always said that she would not ask her father for anything. She had met him once and he had seemed un-interested in her and she said that now he would have to come and find her before there could be any further contact.

The therapist found himself in an impasse. There had been some improvement in the initial flat depression, but no real change in the relationships described. After four years Ms E said in the last session before the therapist's summer holiday that she thought she had better stop and would probably not return after the break. She would write and say what she had decided. The therapist was com-. pletely surprised by this and found himself feeling angry. 'You mean that you intend to just stop, just like that, by writing a letter!' The patient looked surprised: 'Well, I don't like goodbyes.' The therapist thought about this and said he could imagine that sudden endings were the only kind which Ms E knew about but that perhaps a different sort of ending could be considered this time. Ms E went away saying that she would think about it.

The therapist was left with uncomfortable feelings of having resisted the patient's wish to end rather than working with it, and of having failed in the work because

the patient wished to re-enact the ending with her father
rather than working towards an ending in a more considered way. If the therapy ended there, the therapist felt that
he would have to regard it as a failure.

This case illustrates the way in which an ending can be determined
by the pattern of previous endings. It also shows the difficulty for
the therapist in dealing with an ending when he is still playing a
role required by the patient within the relationship. His response to
the possibility of ending is to delay it, and this might well be what
is needed from a therapist: the sudden ending of a therapy that
has reached an impasse may not be the best possible outcome. The
therapist needs to recognise the extent to which he is playing the
required role of the mother who is holding on to her daughter, or
the complementary role of the child whose father will not be close
to her, hoping that the relationship will improve and give her more
of her heart's desire. At the same time, he has to do what is needed
as a therapist in the present.

There are two major schools of thought about such a situation
within the analytic therapies. On the one hand, the therapist is not to
play the role required by this transference but might comment on it.
The therapist in this model would not show any wish or desire to
keep the patient but would merely point out the contamination of the
present by the past. This can be done either by saying to the patient:
'You are treating me as if I were a figure from your past' or by
encouraging exploration of why that particular attitude might be
uppermost. The latter approach is more likely to enable further elab-
oration and understanding because the patient is less likely to feel
criticised for being a child or childish. The purpose for therapists of
these schools would be to relate past memories to the present situation in the hope that the present could be freed from the compulsion
to repeat. This is the approach of what might be called the conflict
school. Deficit models would be more likely to regard making up for
previous deprivation as the priority. Such a therapist might emphasise the need for more therapy as the best thing for the patient in this
situation. Either of these approaches could be combined with an honest assessment of the therapist's own narcissistic involvement in
achieving what would feel like a 'good ending'.

Most models of therapy assume that the past influences the
present, and that pain and suffering arise from memories. Because
of this fundamental problem for humanity we develop defences, and
therefore contentment or equanimity depend on the balance of pain

against defence for any individual. Most therapists are delving into the stories of the past that are brought to them and are interweaving their own thread with all the others. Memories will be produced or suggested. They will be lived through with the therapist and assigned to places where they can either be forgotten or allowed to rest for the time being. The conflict school might encourage the patient to elaborate on the desire to end, whereas the deficit school might be considering either what is missing in the therapy that makes the patient wish to end, or might take the view that deficits have been repaired sufficiently to allow the person to function independently and leave.

The Lacanian critique of both these models might point out that the therapist is working within a required transference relationship which the Lacanian sees as imaginary in the sense that the patient is imagining the therapist through a blindfold of constructed meaning. He is not free to speak for himself but is speaking a language especially developed for speaking to the other that he imagines the therapist to be. We hear about the patient who sees a Jungian therapist and begins to dream in a way that particularly appeals to Jungian methods of working with dreams, and the same might apply to Freudian free association or Rogerian genuineness. This argument leads to a model of technique in which the transference that evolves must continually be dissolved by the therapist who tries to see where it fails or where it becomes false and sterile.

Although there are criteria for readiness to end such as those discussed in Chapter 1, they provide a check-list only, and each therapist will be relying on his own experience of the patient as well as a theoretical model. An ending seems appropriate to many therapists when the patient has become sufficiently like the therapist for the remaining differences to be comfortable. In other words, patient and therapist both perceive the same obstacles in the room. Thus, Ms E had remained different enough to cause the therapist to feel concern that her functioning was not healthy. Therapists who use both conflict and deficit models are looking for something that they can recognise as healthy functioning. Although this may often lie behind whatever are said to be the criteria, therapists obviously need to have a rationale that demonstrates both that they do have criteria and that they are not merely seeking to turn out clones of themselves. If the Lacanian critique is borne in mind, the therapist will always remember the dangers of his own subjectivity and will not court a dependent transference, but will, on the contrary, seek to cut through it to what is still hidden in the unconscious.

The therapist's claim to authority

An important question often asked by the general public and the media is: Why does anyone need a therapist? What can a therapist do that is not done better by a good friend or partner? Two answers present themselves. One is that not everyone has a good enough friend. Many of those who do may not present themselves for therapy because by definition they are not too bad at relationships. On the other hand, therapists have special skills for tracking down what is repressed or forgotten. They do this by listening to what is not said and to what might lie in the gaps, distortions and vicissitudes of what is said and remembered. They are always looking at the residues of the past in order to understand the present.

The therapist is not a perfectly tuned instrument and is affected by his own past and present. If there is a process by which old patterns of thinking and feeling are revitalised to a point where they can interfere with the present, then clearly we would be asking a great deal if we expected therapists to be free of what we hypothesise to be a universal process. The case of Ms E shows that the therapist is not free. The patient, as Searles has pointed out (1965), is an Oedipal love object for the therapist. The patient is a narcissistic object and an object of desire for the therapist, providing scope for the wish to make a difference to someone else and a difficulty to overcome. If the patient is forced to experience his past, repeated in different forms in the present, so is the therapist. Therapists are likely to be seeking their own satisfaction through relationships of this particular one-sided sort. Why else are they therapists?

In spite of the therapist's personal involvement, she does have expertise. Her expertise is in finding and recognising dysfunctional patterns that have been obscured by forgetting. Freud made use of the term *nachtraglichkeit* to convey the idea of deferred action. The child's failures come back to haunt the adult with ghostly imperatives and prohibitions which may no longer have a useful purpose. It is through action deferred to the present, but now dysfunctional, that the therapist can recognise what has once been an obstacle even though there is no obstacle there now. One way of describing what has happened when a pattern survives as a template but without its original reason is to use the concept of *repression.* We know about this also through dreams or through symptoms where the dammed-up memories resurface. This is the way of the neurotic. When memories do not have this form of release, there may be a total cutting off from availability to consciousness as we find in psychosis.

Repression provides a way of preventing oneself from having to be aware of the full effect of trauma such as loss or forbidden desire at the time that it might be felt. Actions may occur which are in effect the deferred results of the original trauma. Because of this, the repression may cause more problems than it is worth, although, like all defences, it is undoubtedly worth something. There are various possible ways of looking at the project of analytic work in this context. We make connections and perhaps some of the hidden patterns or origins of trauma come to light and are remembered. The trouble is of course that any remembering is bound to be a process of revising and altering the original event or events. Each time a memory is activated it will be different. The concept of working through implies that memories which have been forbidden for whatever reason will resurface many times in different forms and will be seeking each time a tolerable context in which to embed themselves so that they can be forgotten rather than repressed. Inevitably, the process of remembering will involve some pain and the patient will wish to avoid pain by cutting off the therapy that is felt to cause it.

A newly qualified therapist when working with a patient who talked about having been sexually abused as an adolescent asked in supervision whether it is necessary that the patient should recount the details of 'what happened'. There was no sign of any wish or intention to do so, and the therapist raised doubts about whether the work could safely be ended because there had been no reference to any detail. This is a difficult question to answer without knowing whether the patient was repressing the memories or had access to them but was choosing not to tell the therapist. If the latter were the case, there might be some point in working to understand the motivation for hiding this from the therapist. Perhaps there is an argument for putting the dilemma to the patient: Is it a problem for you that you have not told me anything more about it, or are you satisfied to leave things as they are?

Adam Phillips sees Freud's unconscious as requiring a continuing process rather than a dramatic purging with an obvious ending. Memories may be allowed to surface from the unconscious:

> Freud is close here to a picture of psychic life that lives in a continual present tense, nothing is forgotten, nothing is deferred, there is just intermittent redescription.
>
> (Phillips 1994: 35)

Such a view of the process of therapy would not be much help in deciding when it might be right to end, as there could always be further scope to modify and improve the redescription. Yet patients and therapists obviously do come to a decision, often jointly and amicably, that it is now a good enough time to end. One of the main forces that enable this to happen may be the ability to give up the infantile imperatives for perfection and the therapist must be able to do this when the patient is ready to do so. The therapy may not be completed, but may be enough for now. In other words, the repetition of the redescriptive process can reach a point where it is tolerable and where it allows for desire and abstention.

Since Freud's model of neurosis implies that what goes wrong and causes psychic pain is a disease of the memory, any device that speeds up the recovery of memories is desirable. Specifying an ending date does seem to speed up the process of therapy in some cases. In this model, a rapid processing of relevant memories would be sufficient if it led to putting together a coherent story of the past as it is now being relived in the present. Once this has been done, we could expect the ego to be strengthened and the patient to be able to think more clearly and make choices. The therapist knows the extent to which this has happened from the reports of what goes on in the real world and, of course, much more reliably, from a difference in the kind of treatment received via the transference. Old dysfunctional patterns of relating will no longer be predominant. Ms E had not managed to remember more than she already knew. Her therapist had not managed to become a large enough force to break through the resistance, and she was able to persist in her current patterns which were held in place by her own version of the past. What changed for her was something external which worked in conjunction with the therapy.

Ms E wrote to the therapist during the break saying that she had decided to return to therapy because she had found a lump in her breast and had to go and have a biopsy. The fear that this induced was insupportable and she realised that she could not do without the therapy. She never said that she could not do without the therapist. The therapist felt very uncomfortable with this reason but was glad that there was to be another chance. The biopsy found no malignancy and the therapy became the place where there was a chance to discover what was beneath the surface. The therapist was able to acknowledge that he had felt

disappointed at the ending because he wanted something
better for Ms E and also for himself. This enabled both of
them to consider how they had needed an external third
element to enable thinking to take place.

Ms E was not only suffering from patterns from the past, she was
also suffering from alienation of her own desire. She had to find an
external event to lead her back to the therapist. She could not find the
need and the wish in herself, but the work that she had done enabled
her to make use of an external event. Once back in therapy she moved
towards greater recognition of what she had been denying: the importance of the person who was there for short periods but who would
take himself off for holidays and was not under her control.

In this view of problems and cure, the problem is said to be
caused by a conflict between the patient's desires and the dictates
of the part of the psyche which seeks to control emotions, particularly the emotions connected with the desire to be loved and to
love, whatever that means to the individual at the time. Because
desire is perceived as a source of pain it is repressed, and a symptom
or neurotic problem will arise. The relation to the therapist will be
distorted by this attempt to avoid pain but the distortion shows the
place where the wound is. The avoidance causes many small
endings. Some patients stop talking before the end of a session.
Some try always to end a session before the therapist does. Some
patients will exercise control, not only at the end of the session but
also by ending their therapy abruptly.

The therapist's subjectivity

For some time, Freud continued his enquiries into the nature of
therapy without looking too closely at the therapist as a subject, not
just a doctor. Other forms of therapy may not accept the hypothesis that the sources of symptoms are unconscious, but most will
accept that something is needed from the therapist that is more than
just the administration of a technique. Freud saw that the doctor
makes therapy possible. The difficulty is that the doctor, however
well analysed he might be, still has his own resistance, his own
repression. In the transference relationship, the therapist is working
with a blindfold over his own eyes so that although he can hear the
words of the patient, he cannot see clearly the person from whom
they are coming; they are filtered through his own net. It therefore
follows that in any therapy, the therapist must be working on the

repressions that defend him from the patient. He must suffer the illness but be able to make some headway towards recovery.

Not letting go: the therapist's use of power

Within the therapeutic relationship, transferred feelings and desires give the therapist power which can be used or misused. Oedipal theory suggests that the patient will need to work out some of his difficulties with the problems of the way the parents used their power. The power of the mother and father may be handed to the therapist in the hope that he can use it well. Even when the therapist's power is great, the patient's own defences may be greater, but a resolution as negotiation or redistribution may be essential.

When Sandor Ferenczi persuaded Freud to take him into analysis, he had only three periods lasting a matter of weeks in each case, between 1914 and 1916. Ferenczi had been called up to serve in the army and was able to come for sessions only when he was on leave. For this reason, he had several periods of intensive therapy; at one time he attended for three hours per day. There was already a powerful emotional link between them and on Ferenczi's side, a strong positive feeling which was clearly recognised as feeling for a father.

When Ferenczi had to return to the army on 9 October 1916, that analysis was declared to be finished, but the struggle that Ferenczi had in accepting the ending illustrates well the difficulty of stopping when there is a powerful transference in full swing. He continued to write letters to Freud so we have an account of his reactions and feelings on stopping and Freud's responses in his letters, usefully summarised in a paper by Judith Dupont (1994). Freud was clearly aware that the analysis had not reached resolution:

You know that I consider as 'finished' your attempted analysis; finished and not terminated; interrupted by unfavourable circumstances.

(Dupont 1994: 309)

Freud then goes on to comment on a love affair of Ferenczi with a woman called Gizella which Freud thought could not possibly work out well. Clearly, Ferenczi was faced with a need to work out for himself an ending to the love affair with Freud as his analyst/father/mother. Ferenczi felt the whole gamut of anger and longing and was aware of the transferential element:

> I must admit that I have got nowhere with my self analysis. It might be that I actually muddled up the situation ... but I must also let work in me untroubled the hostile tendencies towards the father that certainly are existing in me. I am ... fully aware of the transferential character of my reaction to your letter and consciously I am even grateful to you.
>
> (Dupont 1994: 310)

He had asked Freud for just one more session and accused him of trickery in being against the relationship with Gizella. Freud's lack of response to both love affairs was a source of great pain and struggle, but Ferenczi had the advantage of analytic understanding and continued a sort of self-analysis. By Christmas 1916 he was able to write more hopefully:

> Let this sheet of paper be the proof that I have again attained a degree of normality ... I hope that from now on I will be content with less than formerly. I don't want to promise too much ... this will not succeed without relapse ... I am happy to feel grateful once more.
>
> (Dupont 1994: 310)

This last paragraph expresses well the degree of resolution of transference feelings that we might hope for at the end of a brief but powerful piece of work. Ferenczi achieved it by means of his self-analysis and the passage of time. The ability to feel that there is a possibility of being content with something 'less than formerly' might well be another aspect of readiness for termination as well as a realistic assessment of the possibility of feeling worse again. Therapists might regard these as criteria for readiness to end, although there will always be some patients who have to achieve this position on their own once the therapy is over. Gratitude too, as Ferenczi expresses it, if it is genuine and heartfelt is, as Klein pointed out, a most valuable experience, as it mitigates against excessive envy and destructiveness and allows that the therapist may continue to exist independently, and may be at least partly good.

Ferenczi was right in expecting further difficulties. Neither Freud nor he was ready to end. Dupont emphasises that he continued to look for a strong father figure for the rest of his life. He was one of eight children and his own father had died when he was 15. His mother was a strong woman but had difficulty in giving enough time to each of her children. Freud took on the role of father and presumably mother, in some respects, and continued to try to influence Ferenczi, particularly in his work and research. There was much pain in the relationship for both of them. Ferenczi recognised his dependence and his desire for a father, but recognition did not remove the need. The struggle for independence or freedom from this aspect of transference, particularly for Freud, continued until his death in 1933. He had at least acquired the ability to analyse himself and to put his feelings into words, an important benefit, but the story shows us how persistent some aspects of transference can be, and should also remind us that external circumstances that shorten or lengthen therapeutic work must be taken into account.

In the story of Ferenczi, we can see in his urgent and continuing need to have Freud's approval for all that he did, his problem with power and his need for a father figure to be behind him, making him feel stronger than he otherwise could. Most of the models of psychotherapy involve a powerful father or mother with disciples who follow or rebel. This seems to be a universal phenomenon and it is hardly surprising that therapists make their patients go through a process of compliance or resistance. One of the requirements of the Oedipal father is compliance. You must be like me or you must do as I say in order not to be a rival or a threat. This pattern of transference compliance will vary according to the sex of the therapist and whether the patient is a man or a woman, and it may impose a requirement for health or illness, staying or leaving.

In classical Oedipal theory, the child is released only because he submits to the father's rule and goes away first into the busyness of childhood in the latency period and then to find a partner. The girl must give up her love and desire for her mother and accept a man as a substitute for her. The motives for this movement are partly resignation as a response to being deprived of the parents who, in ideal circumstances, have each other, and partly out of fear of punishment: castration or abandonment. This whole process can be seen in the therapeutic situation and of course, for analytic therapies, it is the validity of this analogy that allows transference work to be done. A requirement of the therapist is that he should be totally aware of his role and able to step aside from it so that he does not act it out but merely comments on it. As Lacan pointed out, however, both partners in the analytic couple have an unconscious and both transfer feelings from the past. Can we expect always to be aware? If the complex is, as Freud claimed, connected with the most powerful fears of mutilation and abandonment, how can we expect the therapist to be immune?

If the fear of losing one's own power is a motive for leaving therapy precipitously, the fear of losing the therapist and his loving approval will work in the opposite direction. At some time during any prolonged therapy, the fear of loss and its equivalents in death and dying will be highly likely to emerge. If the work is being done within the transference, the loss that is feared will be the loss of the therapist or the patient in the place of the needed parent. There is no short cut and no way in which loss can be made painless if loving attachment is allowed at all. For some schools of thought, these feelings may not be seen to be connected with infancy, but whether they are seen to be so or not, they will be part of the constellation that surrounds ending. These are the sorts of emotions that are most likely to be hidden or denied:

> Only when the resistance is at its height can the therapist, working in common with his patient, discover the repressed instinctual impulses which are feeding the resistance ... the doctor has nothing else to do than to wait and let things take their course, a course which cannot be avoided or always hastened.
>
> (Freud 1923: 155)

The difficulty of letting go

The greatest difficulty in therapeutic work arises from hidden anxieties about loss. These anxieties may be equally strong for both patient and therapist. Within the therapeutic relationship the therapist concentrates on finding out what causes the most resistance and this shows where the patient's wounds are. If he looks at his own resistance he may discover more of his own. Ira Miller (1965) discusses the anxiety over separation brought about by any thoughts of ending therapy even when there is an agreement to end. He points out that this phase will activate the deeply buried memory of infantile omnipotence when the child tried to hold his parents and prevent them from leaving him by the magic of will-power. At the same time, Miller's patient tried desperately to hold on to the therapist by refusing to give him all the material that he needed. The attempt to tantalise with the possibility that there is more to uncover is another way in which the patient in the grip of the transference resists an ending. The patient demonstrated his need to withhold good things from others through the symptom of *ejaculatio retardata.* Holding back from the climax will be a problem in external relationships and may be susceptible to change in the ending phase, because ending the therapy implies allowing the climax and discovering whether it is equivalent to a loss of one's own good things to the other or whether there is a renewable source that the individual keeps and develops after the end. The whole ending process involves questions about who has the power and whether or not it can be given up or shared.

Much of what has been said already implies the difficulty of letting go for both patient and therapist. Transferred feelings of desire for the one who can repair you or can allow you to repair him hold both patient and therapist in thrall. The therapeutic couple often find that their neurotic needs fit together like a happy marriage. But like most marriages, one partner, hopefully the therapist, is able eventually to move on. The neurotic pattern ceases to be a perfect fit, but there is a possibility for change. In some cases however, an impasse is reached. It may be a contented sort of impasse in which both parties enjoy the therapy and not much harm is done, except that the patient is missing out on other places to put his libidinal attachment.

Patients have many ways of prolonging therapy and other therapists and analysts have written about the technical difficulties of resistance; for example, the silent patient (Coltart 1993), or the patient who acts out and splits himself so that only acceptable parts of himself are brought to the therapy. The therapist's task is always to try to catch out the unconscious self-revelation that will enable the status quo to be shaken a little. The dangers of shaking the tree are of course obvious, in that a patient may be precipitated into a psychotic breakdown or suicide if the tree is shaken too hard. This is why the therapeutic relationship is still important and the old-fashioned values of containment and empathy are not to be despised.

Object constancy

What makes it safe enough for a patient to end? Casement (1985) writes of an object relations view that the therapist constructs a container. The theory of object constancy is another way of looking at the therapist's ability to make ending possible. All therapists emphasise the extent of their availability in the vertical sense of the depth of the contact that is possible in the moment and in the horizontal over the passage of time. They are continually modelling tolerance of separation even though we know that, at times, waiting for the next session is difficult for the therapist if there is anxiety that the patient might not come or, to take one of the worst examples, might have killed himself. Interpretations or interventions may make it apparent that the therapist thinks that separation is not such a terrible thing.

> Dr F is a doctor who has had a very successful academic career and is working her way up the career ladder. She has had a series of passionate sexual relationships with men but the man always turns angry and abusive and leaves her, or drives her to leave him. Recently she has bought her own flat and has not had a man living with her. In one session she says:
> 'I have been in on my own for three nights running. In one way it's a relief to have some peace and quiet, but then I get into a panic that no one will ever telephone me again and I have to ring someone up.'
> The therapist has many choices of response and can of course stay silent here, but thinks this is an important point and so makes an intervention:
> 'Yes, I know that silence or absence means abandonment to you, and it's difficult to wait and trust that a person might be still there when you look again.'

Dr F can begin to hold on to a sense of sufficiency which could be described as object constancy or as the introjection of a good object which is not lost in silence or absence. Hartmann invented the term 'object constancy' in 1952 using Piaget's concept of the need to be able to develop a mental representation of an object in its absence. Hartmann added to the cognitive aspect the need to be able to keep the object as loving. Some of the most difficult therapies centre around the inability of a patient to keep the therapist and his or her words good enough to be useful again the next time. Everyone is familiar with the person who comes back to a session and literally or metaphorically turns to face the wall. The therapist has become hated and bad as the absent object.

The therapist may work with the difficulty of returning to the next session in two ways. She may merely observe the non-verbal effects of habituation and the wordless experience that the therapist remains and is not greatly changed either by the absence itself or by the attacks that have been launched against her by the patient either consciously or unconsciously. In addition it is possible to make interventions that focus on what happens to the image of the absent object and how it is attacked. The therapist who is there to speak has survived the attack and is available to be tested in reality against the damaged therapist that the patient brought with him and from whom he turned away.

Both during the session, through the interweaving of silence and words, rapport and distance, the therapist and patient play the fort-da game, or peekaboo, or whatever we call the learning game that all babies need to play, to prove to themselves that the object can disappear from sight without disappearing from the mind. Akhtar *et al.* (1994) point out that object constancy is closely related to self constancy. After summarising the relevance of the developmental concepts of Mahler (1968) and Winnicott (1965) to understanding how children come to be able to be independent and to survive absence, they conclude that adult psychopathology in such areas as paranoia and malignant erotic transference are connected to a failure in self and object constancy:

> In sum, lack of object constancy impairs the capacities to mourn, tolerate ambivalence and maintain optimal distance. Lacking inner cohesion, such individuals tend to develop compensatory structures leading to paranoia, erotomania, and inconsolable nostalgia. These dynamic and structural configurations have considerable bearing upon the treatment of such individuals.
>
> (Akhtar *et al.* 1994: 449)

Because the therapeutic relationship can embody both therapeutic and developmental processes, there is a possibility that therapy will enable an individual to form more stable self and object representations which will enable the ending process of therapy itself to take place.

Ending by achieving the symbolic

For some therapists, the therapy has been successful if the patient is able to speak his feelings and thoughts to another, whether the other is a part of himself or whether it is the therapist standing in for other possible social relationships. This is a considerable achievement but is only ever partial. The patient can voice his or her reasons for wanting to leave and this ability and willingness to articulate one's thoughts is, of course, one of the criteria for readiness to leave. Words are always addressed to the other whether internal or external and therefore this view of analytic work always implies recognising who is being addressed at any time. When words can be used to communicate, rather than to damage or to confuse, the patient has some hope of being able to process his or her own needs, feelings and desires. If this is achieved, transference, or the imaginary relationship, has decreased. Instead, the needs and demands can be part of a dialogue both internal and with the other in which there are choices.

There is, however, a difficulty. Language is all we have, but in the post-Lacanian world we cannot avoid recognising the inbuilt inadequacy of language. Roger Kennedy writes: 'the unconscious, thanks to language, can speak about the lacking object which shines forth with its very absence' (Kennedy 1986: 180).

Words stand for something which is not the word itself. This implies that language inevitably introduces us into the state of lack or incompleteness that is our lot. Caliban did not thank Prospero for teaching him to speak:

> You taught me language; and my profit on't
> Is, I know how to curse.
> (*The Tempest* I, ii)

There is no guarantee of gratitude from patients either. Lacan's view of language is that it inevitably brings us into the realm of castration, where language hints at what is not known through its gaps and inadequacies. For Lacan, the unconscious 'strives to express what is forbidden to the speaking subject – jouissance and death' (Kennedy 1986: 186). Language in fact is the province of the ego which seeks to ward off the desires of the unconscious and is doomed to remain in an imaginary world. For Lacan, analysis is about the tension between the possibility of some awareness of this hopeless situation and our ability to become a speaking subject who is part of a social order.

Since Lacan terminated his own school of psychoanalysis before his followers were willing to end and without their consent, it is interesting to relate his view of the human subject to the possibility of ending therapeutic work. Achieving the symbolic level by acquiring a language is like achieving a pass in the Ecole Freudienne. It is an initiation but it does not solve the difficulties of being human in any way. The individual has to give up expecting that the analyst or the therapist knows everything and be willing to engage in a dialogue with the other even while knowing that talking can never enable us to reach the truth. Nevertheless, it does achieve something. The French verb *causer* is both to cause and to talk, and the Cause Freudienne which is the organisation that continues to teach and debate Lacanian ideas is therefore carrying on its work in the irony of knowing that the task is impossible.

Language will therefore enable us to try to reach each other but will inevitably frustrate. One possible effect of speech is to allow the subject to define him- or herself: I am this or that sort of person. At the same time it forces us to accept an awareness of human limitations. The other can never know all, whether the other is part of me or you. Desire is infinite and language is all too finite. Ending therapy states the limits of human relationship but it also leaves the possibility of being a little closer to the truth in the future. The habit of talking need not be lost.

References

Akhtar, S., Kramer, S. and Parens, H. (1994) 'The internal mother: conceptual and technical aspects of object constancy', *International Journal of Psycho-analysis* 78: 1046.

Casement, P. (1985) *On Learning from the Patient*, London: Tavistock.

Coltart, N. (1993) *Slouching towards Bethlehem*, London: Free Association Books.

Dryden, W. and Feltham, C. (eds) (1992) *Psychotherapy and its Discontents*, Buckingham: Open University Press.

Dupont, J. (1994) 'Freud's analysis of Ferenczi', *International Journal of Psycho-analysis* 75 (2).

Freud, S. (1914) 'Remembering, repeating and working through', *SE* 12.

Freud, S. (1915) 'Repression', *SE* 14.

Freud, S. (1917) 'General theory of the neuroses', *SE* 17.

Freud, S. (1923) 'The ego and the id', *SE* 19.

Freud, S. (1937) 'Analysis terminable and interminable', *SE* 23.

Hartmann, H. (1952) *Ego Psychology and the Problems of Adaptation*, London: Hogarth Press.

Kennedy, R. (1986) *The Works of Jacques Lacan*, London: Free Association Books.

Mahler, M. (1968) *On Human Symbiosis and the Vicissitudes of Individuation*, Vol. 1, New York: International Universities Press.

Miller, I. (1965) 'On the return of symptoms in the terminal phase of psychoanalysis', *International Journal of Psycho-analysis* 61 (4).

Phillips, A. (1994) *On Flirtation*, London: Faber and Faber.

Sandler, J., Dare, C. and Holder, A. (1992) T*he Patient and the Analyst*, London: Karnac.

Searles, H. (1965) C*ollected Papers on Schizophrenia*, London: Maresfield.

Winnicott, D.W. (1965) *The Maturational Processes and the Facilitating Environment*, London: Hogarth.

3

DEALING WITH ILLUSIONS
Narcissism and endings

I long to see you, hear your voice,
My narcissistic object choice.
(Wendy Cope 1992)

Narcissism can be used to account for a particular kind of imprisonment within the self, manifesting itself in rage or indifference. In this sense it was noted by Freud as a pathology that makes analytic treatment very difficult. The narcissistic character structure describes a state in which it is very difficult to establish a therapeutic relationship. Sudden endings from either patient or therapist are often the outcome. The term has more recently acquired a broader swathe of meaning, extending its range to normal self-interest and self-development. In this sense it has become part of popular culture. By this definition, both patient and therapist are inevitably narcissistic and the therapist will need to recognise and use as constructively as possible his own narcissism.

The narcissistic structure is based on an illusion. Narcissus gazed on the surface of the pool and saw his own reflection, but took it to be that of another. Because of this conviction which the nymph Echo, who fell in love with him, could not shake, Narcissus would not look up and see the real other person who presented herself to him. The narcissistic illusion therefore becomes a delusion if it cannot be changed by the presence of another. The ending of the therapy will remain within the delusional structure unless the therapist can be seen as another and not merely as a projection of some part of the patient's self. The image that Narcissus saw in the pool was incredibly beautiful and he wished to see nothing and no one else. The illusion was maintained with great persistence. He also saw the image in the water as cruel and unresponsive. The patient is most likely to leave when he is projecting the cruel unresponsive aspect of himself on to the therapist, but he may also leave out of a wish to preserve the ideal image unchanged.

This chapter will examine the vicissitudes of the therapeutic relationship when narcissism prevails in either or both partners at the pathological level. Either or both partners will be seeking to preserve their own narcissistic illusion in a way that either prolongs or curtails the therapeutic relationship. At the more normal end of the spectrum, the therapist must make use of his own narcissism to enjoy and value the rewards of the work. This can have a negative side in that the value may be derived too much from the opinions or confirmations of the other. The therapist usually prefers endings to be planned and processed over a long period. This may be for the patient's good. It may also be for the therapist's own satisfaction. The therapist must also experience his own pathological narcissism to work with a patient whose narcissism prohibits constructive relationships.

Freud, in his 'Essay on narcissism' (1914), describes two types of relationships. He defines both by the developmental metaphor. In the first, the desire for food and comfort is satisfied by the mother, and the infant learns to turn first to her and then to others for satisfaction. This he calls the attachment type of object choice. In the second, there is a disturbance of the attachment which might have arisen from satisfactory early relationships and, instead, the individual cannot find others satisfying and turns him- or herself into the only love object. This means that the only kind of relating possible in these circumstances is a search for someone else who will echo love of the self well enough to remove the pain of the early failures. Freud goes on to say that the attachment type of choice is typically the way of relating seen in men and the narcissistic need to *be* loved is typical of women. He does, however, emphasise that these are two types of object choice and that one individual may vary over time in the choices made. Human beings are not divided into two sharply differentiated groups.

The essential question for a therapist is how and whether a particular kind of self-referenced relating can change to something more mutual. Freud used his own observation and also drew on the work of Havelock Ellis in psychology and neurology to arrive at a description of narcissistic relating. He had still not found a satisfactory explanation for the way in which the interest of the individual either stays predominantly focused on the self and images of the self, or moves through a further process towards greater recognition of another. Freud later moved on to distinguish between primary narcissism and secondary narcissism. Lacan criticised this distinction as untenable, since primary narcissism postulates a state in which there is no input from the outside because there is no outside. The infant inhabits a world in which self and other are totally indistinguishable. Lacan asked how the baby could then move to a relationship, even a narcissistic relationship, if there were no way to enter the original closed system.

The illusion of wholeness

For Lacan, the primary human goal is the maintenance of consistency of the pleasurable experiences of bodily satisfaction. These experiences never last and, from its earliest moments, the infant learns the loss that is at the heart of all its pleasure. The infant calls out to the mother only because of the need to maintain pleasure and the awareness of its own lack. Therefore the satisfactions of the body achieved in the earliest moments give rise to a calling out to the other to fill the void that is always opening. Lack is the initiator of the construction of the ego whose purpose is to defend against awareness of privation and loss. For Lacan, the ego holds the organism together in a fiction of wholeness which leads to a turning to others to find the satisfactions or objects of desire which distract from the fundamental lack.

This view of the ego implies an inevitable narcissistic element in relating to others. Such a view leads on from Freud's view of narcissism as a pathology that needs to be cured. For Lacan, it is not so much a curable disease as an inevitable part of the human condition. If this is so, therapy can modify but never cure a narcissistic state. An ending will have to be found from within a more comfortable level of narcissistic need. Therapists are deluded if they believe that they can cure narcissistic tendencies in their patients or themselves. They may well need patients in order to diminish their own narcissism which may be at the normal level, seeking confirmation of the self-image, or they may be at the pathological end of the spectrum in that therapeutic relationships are sought in order to avoid or replace ordinary human relationships.

Being embedded in what is essentially an illusion produces some difficulty. For Freud, both boys and girls begin the history of their love relations by loving themselves. At the mirror stage, the infant catches sight of a delightful image of him- or herself as whole and powerful. There is a joy and a triumph in this perception which is always balanced by the rage and aggression that accompany the hints that it is an illusion. The dependence on the mother which is almost total at this stage is at odds with the perfect body of the

46

imagination. Dependence implies love and need for the mother. Both sexes develop an illusory view of themselves at this stage as being a partner for the mother, based on an unreal wholeness, integration and desirability.

Freud and Lacan were not far apart up to this point, but Freud runs into difficulties because of a more literal view of the importance of the penis as a physical reality rather than for the phallic power which it symbolises. According to Freud, a boy can more easily love someone for being different from his own image, because he is driven, through fear of the father's presence and possible jealous punishment, to give up the desire for the mother and seek her in another woman. The narcissistic option might be to seek his own image in another man. This is a much disputed view of homosexuality. Girls are more problematic even in normal development in Freud's theory because they do not have the fear of punishment (or castration in Freud's terms) as they already lack a penis. Therefore girls will always retain a degree of narcissism, needing to be loved and admired in order to retain the illusory image of wholeness for themselves. This is a much disputed view of femininity.

Preserving the illusion

Mollon (1993) points out that for Freud, both femininity and a certain type of religious belief tend towards the maintenance of a narcissistic structure. If religious belief involves the conviction that one is specially loved and chosen by God and that God is all powerful, this can mean that there is an omnipotent belief in one's own power, safety or rightness. An individual might find that this is a helpful protection and may never bring it to a therapist. On the other hand, if it is brought to therapy, we can assume that it is available for reflection and possible change. There is always an ethical question about whether a particular belief is available for analysis in psychoanalytic or other terms and whether therapy should continue to the point where such matters become an inevitable part of what is considered. Some clients make it very clear that there are areas which are not available for any kind of analysis.

> Mrs G came for ten counselling sessions. She was taking a counselling course and the course requirement was for a minimum of ten sessions. She was just about to finish the training but needed to complete the self-awareness component. She arrived for an assessment saying that she

could see that there was some value in experiencing counselling herself, but she really did not think that she had any
problems. She had a strong religious faith and believed
that God wanted her to help others, perhaps eventually
through ordination but currently through counselling. She
said that she had a loving and supportive husband and
four beautiful children. She pointed out that she did not
wish to discuss her faith or family, but she would be
prepared to look at the difficulty she was having in the
training course.

The therapist was very torn in that this looked like a
hopeless situation as far as any meaningful work was
concerned. On the other hand, if Mrs G was going to be
working as a counsellor, perhaps it was better to embark
on some counselling and see whether what felt to the therapist like a very omnipotent defence could be modified at
all. The therapist was immediately engaged by the narcissistic need for Mrs G to see herself as successful. The
contract was for eight sessions followed by a review after
which she would either leave after a last session or
consider further work.

Mrs G came for the eight sessions during which she
talked about the difficulty she had in restraining herself
from criticising other members of her course who were
behaving in a way that she saw as selfish: 'They just say
what they feel without considering whether they might be
hurting someone's feelings.' She restricted her remarks to
supporting other members of the seminar when they were
attacked and could not understand why her support did
not seem to be welcomed. The therapist suggested that
perhaps Mrs G was wanting to be the person who ran the
seminar rather than being willing to be a member of it which
might have involved acknowledging her own vulnerability.
Mrs G thought about this and said that perhaps she was
quite well suited to lead or to teach but at the moment
she was humble enough to recognise that she had more
to learn.

The therapist was gradually becoming more angry and
frustrated. She experienced a great desire to break the
apparently impregnable sense of rightness that Mrs G was
able to convey. This might not have presented such a
problem if Mrs G had not chosen to train as a counsellor,

although it seems most unlikely that she would have come for any therapy. As it was, the therapist had an ethical dilemma related to the fitness of this client to be a counsellor herself and whether or not confidentiality should be broken. [This aspect of the work will be discussed in subsequent chapters.]

The therapist also had a technical dilemma in deciding how much to challenge the narcissistic problem. Too much challenge would simply lead to a walk out and too little would leave the problem unchanged. The deciding factor was her own anger and frustration which she recognised as arising from her own need to be successful, but decided must be broached, but only in terms of Mrs G's own anger that was not being expressed to the students but was being left to others to express. This anger seemed to relate to the basic narcissistic problem of not being appreciated, which might well be traceable to a repressed experience in childhood with a narcissistic mother. The difficulty was that Mrs G might be left with some of her certainty dented but no time to work it through. Of course, a more likely scenario was that she would be well able to fend off any attempt that the therapist might make to enter her feelings.

In fact, what happened was that the therapist did speak about the possibility of hidden anger in Mrs G that might be conveying itself to other members of the group. Mrs G appeared to be able to accept that possibility and spoke openly about her anger with certain members of the group for not being empathetic enough with those who were being attacked. They were not carrying out God's will that the weak should be supported. This was not, of course, quite what the therapist had been expecting. The time ran out before much more could be done and the result was that Mrs G, perhaps just a little shaken, decided that she would not continue with the counselling for the time being, although she might return at some point 'to hear some more of your very interesting ideas'. The religious attitude conveyed was something that the therapist found difficult to accept, because it seemed to imply such an invincible barrier to any kind of intimacy. It also implied that more powerful help than the therapist could ever provide might be available. This would not in itself be a difficulty if it had not also implied that the therapist was to be allowed very little scope to be effective. Sadly, the short-term nature of the work allowed little opportunity to work with the underlying fear and insecurity.

The religious viewpoint of this patient was embedded in narcissistic grandiosity and illusion. Mrs G might not be able to believe in her own omnipotence but would accept an illusory view of the world, and particularly of death, if both could be dominated by her image of God. An ending that would be satisfactory to the therapist would include some acknowledgement of vulnerability and some lowering of the barriers designed to keep the other person at a prescribed distance. Such a change might have brought with it a different way of seeing God. This, of course, brings us into the realm of the therapist's own narcissism and need to feel that a good job has been done.

If narcissism implies an illusory view of the value of the self, the ending of the therapy with a narcissistic patient would have to achieve some more realistic sense of self-value as well as of the value of others. It might also imply a modification of the nature of religious belief away from a conviction that God specially protects the individual from all adversity. In other words, God could no longer be made the recipient of projections of omnipotence. Religious faith can, of course, vary in the extent to which it places emphasis on certainty and the extent to which it emphasises hope. Hope might well be an element in the ending of a therapy. Total dependence on God and none on man is problematic. Freud's view of narcissistic illusion implies that readiness for ending would require a greater acceptance of external reality and perhaps also an understanding of what is truth. This of course begs the question of how we can expect the therapist or therapist and client between them to come to a greater or better understanding of what is truth. There is a possibility here of an endlessly repeating series of mirrors showing more and more narcissistic illusions, including those of the therapist.

The omnipotent illusion

Religious belief is not, of course, the only way in which an individual can achieve a defensive sense of omnipotence. Kernberg (1974) argued that the narcissistic solution to the dangers and threats of the outside world and to relationships in particular is to create

50

an amalgam of the self with an image of power and strength derived from others. This certainly has an illusional quality to it because it involves a person saying in effect: 'By myself I am weak and vulnerable. I will therefore take my ideal brave, strong, and beautiful and join myself to that. Then I will need no one else and can be totally self-sufficient.'

This creation of a *grandiose self,* as Kernberg calls it, defends against feelings of vulnerability. This inevitably also implies a defence against acknowledging the existence of the other because that might imply a risk of coming back to some sort of dependence. The task for therapy is to struggle with fear and anxiety which the therapist inevitably shares. The therapist must recover first and can often do so only by giving up his own narcissistic investment in being successful. The first time the therapist can allow himself to fail with this patient is likely to be the first time that the patient is able to risk letting some of his own omnipotence go.

The relevance for a theory of ending in therapy is not difficult to see. Given that many of the people whom therapists see come along with some version of a narcissistic problem, we need to look at the way in which the desire to turn oneself into the loved object rather than to allow oneself to love and be loved will have immense implications for the ability to leave the therapist. If a person remains stuck in the narcissistic position, the therapist is needed to fill the role of the one who loves and offers comfort and a feeling of self-worth. Even if the narcissism has allowed development to the point where others are given marginal recognition to the extent that they contribute to the narcissistic needs, there will be great difficulties in relating. No ordinary human partner is likely to offer quite the non-retaliatory, undemanding empathy that a therapist offers. Fortunately, the therapist will fail in other ways and there will be a need to seek other relationships, even if the narcissistic position is particularly resistant to change. The therapist has the constant challenge of showing how he is eliminated from consideration without becoming demanding and critical. If relating remains dominated by demand, and if that is totally split off from being able to love, parting is likely to be sudden and to arise from catastrophic disillusionment, rather than being manageable and bearable.

A problem with seeing and hearing

Threatened by the rage of a narcissistic patient who is too suddenly disillusioned, the therapist may wish to remain throughout the relationship as just the voice of Echo among the mountain caves, gradually dwindling away to silence. Freud believed that it might not be possible to form a useful therapeutic alliance with someone whose relating was of this sort. In the most extreme cases, 'they become inaccessible to the influence of psycho-analysis and cannot be cured by our efforts' (1914). Freud is here speaking of the group of people whom he called *paraphrenics*, who had withdrawn their libido or desire from all people and things in the outside world. Because of this, there was an inevitable inability in these people to respond to influence from the therapist. In order to maintain this position and to sit like Narcissus on the edge of the pool refusing to look at anyone else, the narcissistic individual needs a considerable degree of omnipotence or megalomania. He needs to be able to feel that wishes and desires are extremely, even magically, powerful and can transform reality into the desired shape.

Most therapists sooner or later encounter a client who is not only able to attend, but becomes passionately attached to therapy, yet seems to have no positive feelings about the therapist and is impervious to any kind of change. There are many possible situations in which this kind of stalemate may arise, but clearly we cannot simply wring our hands and say, too bad. Some sort of ending of the therapy must be reached in time and the question is whether it can possibly be constructive in any way. There is a strong and powerful motive to try to understand the difficulty better in order to try to arrive at a resolution. Fortunately in most cases, the impasse is not total. A patient described by Donald Meltzer illustrates the existence of another strand in the psyche of the kind of person who is likely to come to do long-term work. Meltzer describes a man:

> [He dreamt that] he was walking uphill on a lonely woodland track and saw another man about his age, a former business client of very paranoid disposition ahead of him. When the track divided, instead of going to the right as he had intended he followed the other man, going down on to a beach which he recognised as belonging to the village where he had been born and from which he had departed at the age of 6 months when his parents emigrated. On the beach he listened with admiration as the other man declaimed at length about his income and importance, how even on holiday he had to keep in constant touch with his office as they could do nothing without his advice.
>
> (Meltzer 1988: 231)

The business associate was understood as a part of himself that he described at other times as foxy or even as an actual fox who appeared in some of his dreams about a story he had heard as a child. The foxy, narcissistic part was extremely powerful. Simply making conscious what it was like and what it was doing made no difference to it at all. For the first three years of the work, it seemed to grow stronger and increase its hold. This part of the personality also seemed to be involved in a sexual perversion which involved masturbation. Developmentally, Meltzer could make some sense of the perversion as a secret pleasure which could be kept from the patient's mother who was a long-term invalid, and whom the patient cared for in what Meltzer calls a 'custodial manner'.

Nevertheless, even at his worst, we can see that this man had a secret, profound attachment to the therapist. He expressed this partly in an uncanny and disconcerting ability to know things about the therapist. For example, Meltzer describes having borrowed the car of a friend and colleague who lived in a road that the patient traversed in order to reach his session. Although the car was parked out of sight, the patient described a dream in which he saw the house of the colleague with a hole in the road outside, that was just about the size and shape of a car. This kind of connection is disturbing but familiar to all therapists who have worked in depth with such patients. There is no obvious working alliance but there is a deep, often destructive attachment which belies the image of a total narcissism. Even the first dream about the colleague is significant because there is the 'I' of the dreamer as well as the narcissistic colleague who is supposed to be a separate person from the dreamer. What is the 'I' of the dreamer up to, and how will he ever be able to work with the therapist?

In the case described by Meltzer, work was possible and the therapy was not prematurely ended. For a long time the foxy part of the patient prevented him from acknowledging any dependence or love. It kept him impoverished because it denigrated any and everyone else. It allowed love neither of the therapist nor of a woman. Why should anyone submit to such a destructive inner force? The hypothesis that Meltzer puts forward is that if there is no sense of ever having had anyone good, there is bound to be an all-pervading fear. The tyrannical, foxy, businessman aspect of the personality offers some sort of safety because it purports to know the answers. This is what leads it to have an addictive quality. An essential and highly problematic aspect of the therapeutic relationship in this sort of situation is that it has the power and impermeability of an addiction which attempts to force the therapist to stay in the role of supporting the tyrant.

There is an inherent difficulty in working with such a structure. If there is a great deal of fear at the root of the tyrant's power, what is the fear and where does it come from? Winnicott and the object relations school would look at the problem in terms of the mother's failure to meet the infant's gesture sufficiently at the right time. The baby who has to wait longer than it can bear has to develop defences against its rage and distress. If there is too much frustration too soon, the omnipotent defence is developed to deny that there has to be any dependence on an unreliable other. Kohut and the self psychologists have looked at the need for the mother or significant carer to be available as a self object which can gradually move from mirroring to being a separate entity in its own right.

From the writers who have put more emphasis on the development of early infancy as a system in which physical and phantasied inter-action both play a part, such as Klein, Mahler and later Stern, the most significant contribution to the illumination of the problem has been in the area of understanding what happens when there is not sufficient gratification in the phase that Mahler (1968) calls *normal symbiosis*. At this stage the mother and infant form an omnipotent system which provides the safety for the ego to develop and to allow the gradual awareness of the separateness of the other. If this safety is not available for reasons which Klein might see as more constitu-tional and internal and Stern (1986) might see as more interactional, the result is likely to be a tendency to separate the phantasied powerful part of the self, like the foxy part of Meltzer's patient, and the weak, helpless part of the self which cannot make the mother do what is wanted. In the same way, the mother is seen or responded to as if she were either the gratifying mother who does sometimes pro-vide what is needed or the frightening, depriving mother who can-not be controlled. The effort to control becomes paramount and there is no freedom to allow the other person to be him- or herself. The therapist who is playing a part in this struggle will be forced into a position where he has to take some control, at least to prevent dam-age from being done, and the only way out of a repetitive pattern may be an acknowledgement of the impasse to the client. This has the effect of showing that the client is not speaking to a controlling parent, and also shares responsibility for what happens.

Symington (1993) emphasises the part played by the infant and child in what goes wrong for the adult. His point of view is valu-able in clinical practice in that he points to the choice of the narcissistic person to turn away from the life force. This can be seen in physical terms as a refusal to take the breast or the nipple when it is offered; a useful metaphor to describe the sense in which the person refuses all offers of the symbolic feeding provided in therapy. The fear is that choosing to take what is offered will lead to much greater disappointment and abandonment. This leads us back to the difficulty in working with such clients. Any acceptance of hope and the value of what the therapist is offering inevitably strengthens the resistance because the potential loss is greater. We then have the impossible situation of working with someone who hates and envies the therapist for having good things and does not recognise that anything is given, and yet is quite unable to tolerate absences, ends of sessions or holidays.

The thought of the ending of therapy cannot be tolerated with ordinary mixed feelings. An impending disastrous end may always be present as a threat. For some people the threat is seen to be coming from the therapist: 'I know you want to get rid of me.' It may be felt to belong to the foxy, controlling, businessman part of the patient denying any love or care for the therapist. Such a person may often speak of his intention to leave the therapy because it is not useful or is said to be doing positive harm. The harm may be imagined as being in the mind of the therapist who is seen as omnipotent and using his power for evil purposes. This can be clearly seen as a projection of the omnipotent part of the patient which is then perceived as if it were in the therapist. Unfortunately, of course, with these patients, we are all much more inclined to act in the way that we are being seen and to become unduly powerful, make mistakes and become harmful. This situation enables the patient to feel justified in maintaining the tyrannical part of himself in order to protect him from the threatening therapist. Quite often such a situation is resolved only by a sudden, apparently catastrophic ending in which the patient leaves and the therapist never knows what he takes with him. The patient perhaps seeks to convince him- or herself that anger is justified and that of course it is felt at the time to be preferable to the vulnerability of dependence.

Because the unduly narcissistic person tries so hard to maintain the status quo, endings are likely to be problematic, not only because they may be made too soon, but also because there is often very little sign of any change.

Mr H, a man of 35, had been seeing a therapist for several years. He had made some progress in his work situation where he had been successful in a promotion and his relationships with his colleagues had improved. His relationship with the therapist remained static however. It was not difficult in any way. He seemed to be prepared to continue to attend sessions once a week, describe his week at work and go away again.

This began to worry the therapist, who was aware that relationships outside work were not good. Mr H was describing homosexual and heterosexual encounters but they were ephemeral. His main satisfaction came from masturbating in front of a mirror. He was willing to engage in various attempts to understand this, first in terms of his fear of women and his powerful and rather frightening mother. Second, it was seen to relate to his desire to internalise his father who had been absent for much of his childhood and had died when he was 10 years old.

The trouble was that the interpretations seemed to be well received, and he left each session better than he arrived in that he always began slow and depressed. For a long time this kept the therapist going, but gradually she began to be aware that what was happening was circular and was showing no sign of any change. The conclusion was that the sense of impasse should be presented to the client. Mr H accepted this with interest, but again it seemed to sink without trace. As a result, the therapist decided that she had to make herself a real person rather than a part of the patient's fantasy as the watcher. In order to do this and to make a difference, she decided to set a date for ending the therapy. This was met with shock and distress that went on for several weeks in the form of silent misery or indirect anger. The ending was difficult for both because it was not possible to pretend that a great deal had changed. Nevertheless, there was a degree of strength in the way in which the patient eventually accepted that the therapist was determined that the ending should take place. Coming up against this reality caused both mourning over the loss of the ideal therapist and eventually enough anger to set some hope going.

When the therapist overcomes her narcissism enough, an ending may be possible. Nina Coltart (1997) in her last book *The Baby and the Bathwater* wrote that she feared that training analysis or therapy makes therapists more rather than less narcissistic. Why should this apply more to trainees than to anyone in therapy? The obvious, if superficial, interpretation would be that many years of compulsory self-observation required in most training induces a habit of gazing inward and looking at one's own responses to all interactions. This might well be the case, although one would hope that the inward looking would result in a self-examination in relation to another rather than an inability to look at the other.

Nevertheless, the therapist's own narcissism is bound to be an element in any therapeutic relationship. It leads to two main groups of responses to clients. In the first group, the therapist needs to compel gratitude and appreciation from the client. This is in order to obtain the sense of life from an image which reflects back to the needy therapist: 'Yes, you are a good therapist, you are worthwhile, you are loved, you are desired.' this is an emotional bond that is felt to be needed and therefore the therapist does not let go of clients and is blind to indications of a reasonable need to end. The second group is more sophisticated and has recognised the difficulties inherent in the obvious narcissistic satisfactions being sought by the first group. These therapists are inclined to exaggerate their independence of the client and to become oblivious of the client's efforts to be connected.

The following cases show the sorts of situations that can arise:

Ms J had been seen by a psychodynamic counsellor for over two years. She had worked through considerable difficulties in her relationship with her partner, had become much more accepting of his emotional limitations and was prepared to enjoy what he had to offer. At the same time, she became much more relaxed with the counsellor and was able to accept the counselling sessions and say that they were useful to her. She felt that she had benefited greatly but as she was not in paid work and had two small children, the fee was difficult to find. She talked about one of her children reaching the end of primary school. She had enjoyed the experience greatly but was now ready to move on and was excited, if a bit anxious, about the new possibilities at secondary school.

The counsellor said that she understood that J was ready to move on from what she had been working on to a new area and that there were perhaps things in her childhood that she had not yet discussed. Perhaps they were exciting but also frightening to contemplate. J was surprised by this and said, no, she really did not think there was anything else that she needed to work on and that actually she was contemplating making an ending in about six weeks' time. She added that the fee was rather difficult to find and she could not go on indefinitely, although she did enjoy the sessions. The counsellor was shocked by this and said that they would have to talk about it the following week.

When J arrived for her next session, the counsellor was looking much happier and J thought with relief that the ending might be easier than she had feared. The counsellor began the session by saying that she had been thinking about what J had said last week and was very concerned indeed that J might leave prematurely because she could not afford the fees. She had therefore arrived at the idea that J might like to do some work instead of paying the fee. The counsellor had a large garden and thought that J might be able to work for two hours in the garden in order to earn an hour of therapy. With this issue out of the way, they could both concentrate on what was preventing J from being able to talk about what was still bothering her. J was very surprised at this but said that if the counsellor thought so, perhaps she did have some more work to do and agreed to the proposal. The ending was not mentioned again for some weeks. When it was mentioned again, J said that she was very unhappy with the counselling, did not know what the counsellor expected from her and did not wish to work in the garden any longer. At this point the counsellor became angry, saying that J needed to learn to experience gratitude. After this session, J did not return and the therapy ended in anger on both sides.

The problem in this situation is caused partly by the therapist's no doubt genuine wish to encourage the client to continue to explore her own experiences at school and perhaps to illuminate her relationship to her daughter's experiences further. Unfortunately, this is not justified by the client's account of external circumstances, nor is it clear within the relationship to the therapist that there was any urgent need for the patient to do further work. The counsellor was the one who could not let go.

The therapist's readiness for the work to end cannot be taken as a criterion for ending if the therapist is not sufficiently aware of his own narcissistic need to have the client continue to attend sessions. In this case, the therapist wanted the client to be in the role of gardener. This might seem to be perfectly sensible because the client was good at gardening. Following Voltaire's conclusion to *Candide* where the ultimate good was seen to be the acceptance of the need for all of us to be content to work in the garden, there is philosophical justification for seeing some health in the reality and symbolism of gardening. Nevertheless, in psychodynamic or psychoanalytic work, this situation is not healthy because the client was going to be working for the therapist and this means that the therapist was in a position of control and power which is totally unacceptable in conjunction with the continuing therapeutic relationship. Inevitably there would be potential for the therapist to approve or disapprove of the work done and for the client to cheat or work extra hard. This could lead to all sorts of muddles because these real problems would be ongoing, created by the therapist's action, and would need to be resolved through negotiation. In every therapeutic relationship valuable work can be done when real mistakes are made or difficulties arise. Nevertheless, the therapist seeks not to introduce his or her own material because that may need more work than the client's problems. Some therapists might disagree with this conclusion and would feel that such a problem based in reality could provide valuable therapeutic experience.

The opposite attitude towards clients is demonstrated by the therapist who has no need of clients at all in his or her own mind. When a client mentions ending, this type of therapist is inclined to greet the move with enthusiasm as a sign of growth and autonomy. The enthusiasm may well hide a deeper need which is disguised even from the therapist. This attitude may make it easier for the client to leave, if prematurely, but it may also lead to aborted endings where the client has to keep returning in the hope of getting the therapist to show some warmth and desire. Very often a client tests out the therapist's willingness to let him or her go, in the hope that an early experience of indifferent parents can be changed into a knowledge of being wanted. The experience of not being wanted in the first stages of development may have been illusory of course, and the task of the therapist in the case of the client who is testing out his or her welcome is to make clear that not knowing the therapist's mind but deciding to go or stay without that reassurance is still possible.

Since Lacan, we have had a much more sceptical view of the possibility of achieving a relationship with the other that is free of narcissistic illusion. At the point at which the client or the therapist decides that the work should end, each has to recognise some of the illusory nature of the relationship to the other. In the more extremely narcissistic patient or therapist, the illusion of a pleasing self will have been maintained by the presence of the other and it will be much harder to maintain without the reflection that has been provided. The ending process itself will perhaps allow for some of this need and distortion to be addressed.

References

Coltart, N. (1997) *The Baby and the Bathwater*, London: Karnac.

Cope, W. (1992) *Serious Concerns*, London: Faber and Faber.

Freud, S. (1914) 'Essay on narcissism', *SE* 14: 67.

Kernberg, O. (1974) 'Further contributions to the treatment of narcissistic personalities', *International Journal of Psycho-analysis* 55: 215–240.

Mahler, M. (1968) *On Human Symbiosis and the Vicissitudes of Individuation*, New York: International Universities Press.

Meltzer, D. (1988) 'Terror, persecution, dread, a dissection of paranoid anxieties', *International Journal of Psycho-analysis* 49: 396–400.

Mollon, P. (1993) *The Fragile Self*, London: Aronson.

Stern, D. (1986) *Interpersonal World of the Infant*, New York: Basic Books.

Symington, N. (1993) *Narcissism, A New Theory*, London: Karnac.

4

STAYING ALIVE

The patient's unilateral ending

Be absolute for death. Either death or life
Shall thereby be the sweeter.
(Shakespeare, *Measure for Measure* III. i)

If therapy is valuable, why do people not stay until a mutually
agreed ending can be achieved? Unfortunately, the desirable length
for a therapy is a subject on which therapists and patients often
disagree. This chapter will look at the ways in which patients take
charge of the ending process, in opposition to the view of the therapist. Occasionally therapists do harm and in such a case it is only
the patient who knows this and must make an ending (Murdin 1995).
Usually, patients and therapists are able to arrive at a joint agreement over ending but when there is a sudden or apparently
premature end, therapists do not find it easy to work with a patient's
unilateral decision. If the patient allows any time to the therapist at
all, she must ask questions: is it right for this patient at this time
or is it the result of inadequate work on the part of the therapist?
Therapists often do not know the answer and have to accept the
discomfort of not knowing. This chapter will examine some of the
theoretical and practical background for patient-determined endings
and some of the ways in which therapists handle them in practice.

Patients may be driven to leave by the working of the death
instinct or by their desperate clinging to life as it is. There are three
emotional states which predominate when patients leave therapists
without agreement: they leave in anxiety, they leave aggressively,
and they leave in silence. Each of these endings presents the therapist with a different problem to solve, because each is a different
version of the refusal of the awareness that therapy offers.

Ending is closely connected with dying at conscious and unconscious levels. One of life's most difficult tasks for all of us is to
face personal death. Ending long-term therapy creates a microcosm

of an individual's way of dealing with his own dying and his defences against it. Most people find the helplessness of dying to be one of its most frightening components, and face it with anxiety, with anger or with silence. Ending therapy, like dying, involves giving up the possibility of total control of the other person. The patient may begin in a state in which he or she is so afraid of what other people do that the only hope seems to be to control. A successful therapy may be one in which this need for omnipotent control has lessened enough to allow a mutual decision and the possibility of the other person going his or her own way. A unilateral ending is still an attempt at total control. Either the therapist has to be eliminated, or those parts of the self that the patient cannot tolerate must be silenced by ending the therapy that threatens to give them a voice.

This exercise of power relates very closely to the view that human beings have a tendency that pushes and pulls them towards death. Both Freud and Lacan have written of the concept from different angles and most other theorists, notably Melanie Klein, have taken a stance on whether or not there is an impetus towards death and self-destruction. Klein added the vitally important idea that envy is the deflection outwards of the feelings of hate and destructiveness. It is a universal and powerful force which is potentially responsible for destructive endings. The patient may envy the therapist his knowledge, or his calm or all the good things which he possesses in the patient's fantasy. In Klein's view this envy is omnipresent and leads to continuous attempts to subvert the therapy (see e.g. 'Envy and gratitude', 1957: 184). Alternatively it may lead to the destructive catastrophic ending. When envy is operative, the patient may prefer to deprive himself of the therapy that he needs rather than allow the therapist the satisfaction of doing good work and reaching a planned ending.

Envy is generally recognised to be a powerful force but even many followers of Freud have rejected his concept of the death instinct, for example, 'Freud's tortuous formulations of the death instinct can now securely be relegated to the dust bin of history' (Sulloway 1992: 394). Lacan's critique of the concept has shown that it is still of explanatory power when we try to understand the patient's devotion to his suffering.

For Freud, death was equated first with the biological tendency of all living cells to age and to return to an inanimate state. He hypothesised that such an instinct must exist in the psychological make-up of man as an animal and as a collection of cells. Later he developed the view that there is a drive towards death and destruction which is potentially equal and opposite to the drive towards life. The aim of the death drive is to achieve stability, calm, peace. It is the force that leads to repetition, conservatism and maintaining all sorts of counter-productive but familiar situations. It may lead to an attempt to force the therapist into compliance and maintaining the status quo or it may lead to abandoning a therapy that is working only too well. The life force can be seen as leading towards change and development. The strength of each force varies in each individual.

Very often, a sudden unpredicted ending is a repetition of a pattern of sudden endings or abandonment in which the therapist is unwittingly or unwillingly playing a familiar (to the patient) role. Ending in this view is an attempt to maintain the stability of the familiar even if that is painful and counter-productive. From Lacan's point of view, devotion to pain, or the symptom, is caused by the death instinct working through *jouissance*: the irreducible need to suffer that lies at the depths of the unconscious: Ragland relates this closely with Freud's position:

> Freud found chaos in what one could not control and called it negative transference or unconscious masochism. Lacan viewed masochism as a symptom of fundamental displea-sure, discontent, even perverse enjoyment, in the breach of the pleasure principle that places a stubborn obstacle in each person's life and a malaise in civilisation. Yet the malaise or lack in being or want to be lingers because it is structural.
>
> (Ragland 1995: 92)

In other words, for each of us there is a terror of the void or lack in us and we trap ourselves in familiar suffering so that we do not have to see it.

For Freud, repetition of patterns of behaviour or relating fulfilled the need to maintain stability and consistency and therefore he linked them more positively to the seeking of pleasure. Stability and consistency are preferable to the pain of awareness, but even here there is a problem because what is seen as self-indulgence leads to guilt. Anything that can be felt as pleasurable must be hidden. The therapist is often not allowed to know what has been satisfying in the therapy for this reason.

For Lacan, repetition of counter-productive patterns of behaviour is a sign of the working of the unconscious attachment to one's own suffering. Because it is so deadly to continue to repeat what is painful, the therapist should try to show how the patient is caught in networks of repetition. These repetitions contain in them the fossilised remains of old family myths and desires, but not the desire of the patient. If we can gain some inkling of this, there is a possibility of freeing the patient who otherwise continues to struggle within the historical need to maintain the status quo both for himself and for the other, however negative that might be. Therapists of course have the problem that both ending and not ending can be ways of maintaining the status quo. Patients are trying to show what they are, and at the same time attempt to hide their tracks. The therapist also has an investment in the status quo; this will be considered further in Chapter 5.

May I go now?

Although some patients leave therapy in anger or dissatisfaction, the great majority make a plan to leave and often ask the therapist's view before making a decision. The former may tax the therapist's judgement and tolerance but the latter case is even more difficult. The therapist might experience the question as continuing dependence that requires more work or as part of a healthy autonomy. Consulting the therapist about her view may be seen either as lack of confidence in the patient's own judgement or as a rational desire to have the whole picture available before making a decision. If we accept that the therapist's own feeling about the potential ending is one of the most reliable indicators of readiness to end, we can see that two different patients asking the therapist's view about readiness to end might use exactly the same words in each case, but for one they might indicate that the patient is ready to leave, while for another it is too soon. The only detectable difference will be in the therapist's internal response to the level of anxiety from which the request arises.

Consciously, the neurotic patient may try to work with the therapist and to achieve a constructive ending at the right time. The anxiety at facing one's own pain may be concealed beneath a veil of rationality. At the beginning, the patient who has no knowledge of therapy or analysis has no idea what sort of time scale will be useful. Stories in the media emphasise the possibility of exploitation: therapists just want to hold on to patients for the sake of the income they provide. Of course there is an element of truth in this. The world of therapy is no different from any other in that it is dominated by economics, and the economics dictate that there is a limited number of people seeking therapy at any given time. Therapists are not allowed to advertise according to current Codes of Ethics and therefore they must wait for patients to present themselves via self-referral or the referrals of colleagues, family doctors, etc. This inevitably produces a climate of some uncertainty. In the early stages of a career there is a need to seek work and the temptation to try to hold on to people can be strong.

Patients have equal and opposite conscious motives for wanting therapy to end. Developmentally, leaving home implies adult status and independence. Therapy may be costing a great deal of money. It may be interfering with work, time with family or just involve tiring journeys. Logic and rational thought imply that therapy should end as soon as possible. Judging the degree of anxiety that tells of suffering beneath the surface is a skill that therapists must acquire in order to form a view about when a patient needs help to end, and when the right thing is to continue to try to interpret the ending as an attempt to escape from anxiety.

External reality

Therapists whose model emphasises the internal world of the patient often have problems with recognising external reality. Many therapists would say that the job of the psychotherapist is to interpret what the patient brings and therefore there is no need to pay any attention to external reality. The therapist makes clear what is the fee, what are the hours and when and how long holidays will be. Beyond this, he or she has no concern with the realities of the patient's life. In his biography of Winnicott (1986), Adam Philips describes a meeting of the British Psycho-analytical Society during the war. While the meeting continued, bombs began falling outside. Winnicott, who could recognise external reality even if it had not been crashing about his ears, drew the attention of the meeting to the air raid. He was ignored, and the meeting continued as if nothing were happening. Therapists can be very good at ignoring the limitations imposed by such realities as lack of money or a long journey.

At the other end of the spectrum are the therapists who will try their best to accommodate the reality needs of their patients. For example, what happens if a patient tells the therapist that he or she can no longer afford therapy? This sort of potential ending may arise as a result of the patient or a partner losing a job. It may also be caused by separation of partners or by a patient voluntarily giving up a lucrative but hated job because the therapy has enabled greater courage and freedom in choosing. Does the therapist then allow the patient to attend for a lower fee, or simply say nothing and allow the patient to end? (See also Chapters 7 and 9). I have often heard it said that if a patient really wants therapy he or she will find the money somehow.

> Ms K told me that in her twenties she had gone to London, taken a job as a cleaner and stayed there for three years in a squalid bed-sitter in order to have analysis there. Reduced fees were not available. Although she had a university education, she had no place on a career ladder and had not yet acquired dependants.

In fact, Ms K needed the help of analysis in order to be able to achieve those things. The situation would have been different if she had had dependent children or a place in a career already. Her analyst would not reduce his fee and she would have done without the help that it undoubtedly gave her.

There are many people who are in the middle of therapy but have changes of circumstances. Each therapist must decide whether or not to continue at a lower fee or to try to work with the ending that these circumstances impose. This may well involve anger and disappointment that the therapist is not willing or able to be the rescuer. This situation is particularly difficult if it occurs in the middle of long-term therapy. The arguments for continuing may be strong both for the well-being of the patient and for the therapist's own satisfaction, but therapists, like other professionals, are not obliged to continue with a patient who cannot afford to pay.

Therapist exploitation

Of course there are other situations in which it is necessary or desirable for the patient to leave. Unethical behaviour, most obviously the therapist's inability to control sexual attraction to the patient or emotional exploitation may cause the patient to flee. That therapists abuse patients sexually and also in other ways is incontrovertibly true. Samuels writes:

> What we know from the psychological study of incest is that when one meets a universal moral taboo, with which

everyone in a culture seems to agree, one is probably in the presence of universal impulse.

(Samuels 1999: 150)

Samuels makes the point that public concern over the sexual behaviour of therapists, usually but not always male, is justified and should also be the concern of the profession. Patients who are being abused often may not be able to leave because they are enmeshed in the web woven by their own desires as well as by the therapist's desire. Samuels adds:

Relationship not orgasm is the secret goal of the sexually aroused patient. Power not orgasm is the secret goal of the sexually active male analyst as he replicates the power relations between men and women in our culture.

(Samuels 1999: 153)

How can there be safe analytic work in which a patient will never be caught in a net of abuse nor forced to flee prematurely in order to be free? Samuels makes the useful point that there can be no wholly safe way of working with sexuality. Perhaps the recent emphasis on mother and baby of the object relations school has encouraged a denial and therefore an acting out of sexuality in the therapeutic relationships. Samuels advocates a somewhat enigmatic stance which is *neither literal nor metaphorical* (Samuels 1999: 154). The difficulty of achieving safe therapy, like safe sex, is that there is no such thing, and in each therapeutic partnership the therapist will have to work out a new resolution of desire versus self-denial. Female therapists may not be as prone to abuse their patients sexually as males but they *are* more prone to the emotional exploitation of the mother who cannot let her child go and who exercises all sorts of emotional manipulation to keep the patient who fulfils her narcissistic needs. In this sense, she too seeks power. If the therapist cannot recognise this impulse and find a way of working with it, the patient must be helped to leave and find another therapeutic relationship in which to seek a resolution.

Sometimes, however, patients leave because of the fear of their own unethical behaviour. A male patient may find his erotic feelings about a woman therapist very difficult to accept because he is afraid that he could carry them out through his superior strength. Therapists owe it to patients to make sure that the setting in which they work is safe and that the patient knows that it is. Thoughts and feelings can then be expressed without there being danger in reality. There will always be danger in (ph)fantasy. Almost any unacceptable feelings of murderousness or sexuality may arouse such shame and guilt that the patient chooses to leave rather than risk revealing them. Therapists can do no more than try to guess when there are such feelings and make them available to thought and words.

Patients may leave out of fear of breakdown. Winnicott's well-known paper (1986) points out that this is essentially fear of a breakdown that has already happened. Nevertheless, the grip that the ego has on reality is always tenuous, and patients may be right in fearing being overwhelmed by the unconscious if they give it a chance to surface. Winnicott calls it the search for 'personal non-existence' (1986: 181) and he points out that it is connected with the need to experience emptiness. Emptiness is necessary as a prerequisite to filling. There cannot be hunger for food or new experiences until emptiness is accepted and lived through. Premature ending may relate to the fear of emptiness and to the inability to survive the experience of it when it occurs again in therapy.

Therapists may be much more insouciant than patients about the risks, but must recognise that the cost of therapy to an individual may be more than financial. Some patients leave in order to avoid breakdown or the collapse of a carefully constructed defensive framework that keeps them functioning at least adequately. Therapists may wish to see their patients through such a breakdown because they are confident that the patient will emerge in a better state at the other side, but the patient does not share this belief. Moreover, the patient does not know that there is a way through. The effect of an intransigent therapist will certainly be to produce an angry patient even if the patient had not been overtly angry in the first place. There might be much to be said for making the anger overt, but the therapist who lets a patient leave in a rage of mis-understanding is allowing himself to be such a bad object that the earlier work of the therapy may be spoilt or wasted.

The patient is seeking an experience that is worthwhile in itself while it lasts and that seems to hold some hope of a better life in the future. Rosemary Dinnage, in her anecdotal account of a number of therapies (she interviewed forty patients and printed the accounts of twenty of the forty in her book *One to One* (1988)), found that out of twenty interviewees, a few were angry and disappointed, a few were deeply impressed and grateful and the majority had mixed feelings about the therapy they had received. Dinnage's conclusion is that therapy is a process and that the process must be worthwhile.

The patients were not necessarily seeking an experience that would be easy or pleasant, but they needed to feel that it was a movement or a progression. The image of a journey is often used. In many cases the process is enjoyed in its own right, so much so that sometimes the end of the journey is avoided for that very reason. It is sometimes better to travel than to arrive.

The patient is also seeking satisfaction, which may well be derived from something that is challenging and allows for deep feeling. Veronique, one of Dinnage's interviewees, points out that she was dissatisfied with her first therapist, whom she left because he did not probe or penetrate deeply enough. With him she was able to get away with her persona and her false self. This had led to a therapy that was comfortable and supportive but not deeply satisfying. Here again we are faced with the problem of deciding at the beginning whether the process will be sufficiently satisfying to justify the difficult parts and the lack of enjoyment that will inevitably be part of a long and deeply experienced therapy.

Substitute satisfactions

Anna Freud wrote on 'Acting out' in 1968. She cites Freud's view of 'the compelling urge to repeat the forgotten past and to do so within the analytic setting by actually reliving repressed emotional experience transferred onto the analyst and also to all other aspects of the current situation' (Freud 1968: 166). Wishes and desires are being held in check by neurotic behaviour which disguises them, but the wishes are always striving to make themselves felt. There is a constant threat to the balance that has been achieved. In therapy, the balance is threatened by the actions and words of the therapist. She points out the essential difference between the aims of the therapist and those of the patient within this paradigm:

> struggles between analyst and patient ensue due to the fact that in the analyst's intention, this re-living of the past is meant to increase remembering while from the aspect of the patient's id it has one purpose only: to attain belated satisfaction for formerly frustrated strivings and to do so via the appropriate actions.
>
> (Freud 1968: 166)

This view of mental functioning implies that the patient comes to therapy to attain satisfaction that will substitute for the satisfactions lost or denied to the child that the patient once was. Substitute satisfactions do not allow a full life but preserve a minimal living. The analytic therapist, on the other hand, is not setting out deliberately to give those satisfactions but to encourage the patient to be conscious of the desire so that the underlying wishes and needs can be verbalised and the anxiety faced and lessened. This is as far as therapy goes because the patient is then left with the need to accept those unmet needs in consciousness and to get on with living in the light of that truth but without too many neurotic substitute satisfactions. If this is accepted as the therapeutic situation, it will obviously lead to strife and disharmony at times as the patient seeks satisfaction which the therapist does not, or probably cannot give. Acting out in this view is the way in which the patient tries to achieve such substitute satisfactions as attacking the therapist in the form of a friend or relative, or achieving substitute erotic satisfaction from promiscuous sexual encounters.

Satisfaction can be achieved from almost any emotion along the gamut from masochism to sadism, from idealisation to hatred. Anxiety can be assuaged by any form of defence but in the ending process it is noticeable that patients may be so successful at concealing their fears even from themselves that they appear totally calm and rational, congratulating the therapist on having been helpful. The only recognition of the underlying state comes through the therapist's own feelings. Can the therapist be trusted to distinguish anxiety that is a response to the patient from that which arises from more selfish motives?

Other patients provide a more overt agenda in that they react with fury to their internal pain and often to mistakes made by therapists reacting badly under their attack. Commonly such patients threaten ending before they leave. Therapists deal with such attacks from their patients in various ways, one of which of course would be to retaliate in order to satisfy their own hatred and sadism. Some prefer masochistic satisfactions and will put up with anything. Training, along with the therapist's personal analysis, is intended to minimise this. A potentially more constructive response is to make a theory about destructiveness, calling it, for example, 'negative transference'. If patterns of behaviour can be seen to be repeated or attempted, the patient may be helped by seeing the patterns. The therapist too is helped by having a name for what is happening and an explanation for the attacks that may well continue for long periods. Threats of imminent leaving seem to the therapist like a manifestation of the death instinct. Repetition seems like a dead weight.

Cycles of threat followed by a grudging continuation may need what Symington (1986) called the 'analyst's act of freedom'. After a long impasse he managed to see that he was disregarding his patient's potential for change and development. His disregard had been expressed by allowing her to continue to pay a low fee. This emotional deadness had held both of them in a repetitive groove. When Symington was able to move, the whole course of the work changed. If the therapist cannot find some life in this way, the patient may commit an act of freedom which will turn out to be destructive.

Some therapists may well seek to excuse bad work blaming it on the patient's envious destructive instinct. On the other hand, all therapists are likely to encounter sooner or later the patient whose thinking and reflecting function is so unreliable that he is not able to respond to what is being offered or to ask for something different with anything other than hate and acting out. The acting out may take the form of missing sessions or of being late for sessions. Either of these may be interpreted or occasionally ignored by the therapist, because, if anything, they make the therapist's life easier, and therefore the therapist is tempted to let them continue. More problematic is the patient who creates a noisy disturbance or refuses to leave at the end of the session time. The refusal may be confined to the small delays of putting on clothes, finding car keys, going to the lavatory, etc. It may take the form of sadistic behaviour to relatives, friends or work colleagues. It may be easy to ignore because it may be carefully separated from the relationship with the therapist. If these communications are ignored, they may escalate until there is a furious outburst in which the therapist can stand no more or the patient leaves.

Predicting problematic endings

A careful look at some examples of patients' behaviour in ending therapy shows that it relates closely to the kind of problem the patient brings in the first place. If we could assess accurately, we might be able to estimate the kind of ending that a patient would seek and to work with that in mind. Insofar as the projected ending might be a repeating pattern of impulsive behaviour that cannot be thought about or negotiated, it might well display the pathology that the patient is coming to discover and change. Of course, one of the aims of assessment is to discover what the patient does wish to do in therapy, so that the patient's wish can be considered as part of the whole picture. Unfortunately, assessment in psychotherapy is still a very inexact science. Many therapists would deny that it is a science at all, preferring to see it as an art in that every patient is unique and no laws can be deduced that will not eventually become strait-jackets preventing or limiting creativity and humanity in treatment. Nevertheless, trends in patterns of feeling and behaviour can already be discerned even with the limited longitudinal studies that are currently available.

One way to anticipate the kind of ending that a particular patient might shape for himself would be to think in terms of psychopathology. I have already discussed the acting out of the patient who has difficulty in containing his own anxiety sufficiently to continue in therapy. Does a hysterical patient seek a different kind of ending from that of an obsessional person? Does a depressive tend towards a different process from that of the phobic? Certainly they need different responses from the therapist.

The hysterical patient

If hysteria implies a bodily expression or enactment of a sexual problem, a hysterical patient will approach intimacy with a need to achieve a sexual relationship, but will break it off before there is a risk of his or her true involvement. In this way, anxiety is allowed to rise to a point that is felt to be bearable and then suddenly cut off before it can damage the patient. This is the pattern that will be repeated in the therapy in various ways and will tend towards a sudden and unexpected ending just when the therapist least expects it. Dora is one of Freud's best known cases. She has been made into a heroine by feminists because she loved another woman and kept her love secret while Freud exercised his male mind on the various combinations of males desired and desiring that entered her story. Dora walked out on Freud, simply leaving after one session and refusing to return. Appignanesi and Forester (1992) in their book on Freud's women say, however,

> the way in which Dora walked out on Freud is not unambiguously the victory of her desire for self determining solitude . . . but her departure may not have been so much the incarnation of the revolt of women forced to silence but rather a declaration of defeat. For Dora to have truly succeeded we would have to have seen her finding the promised land that can be glimpsed through her story, the adorable white body of her loved one and her own feminine silent

body, the body that lies beyond the phallic world of Oedipal triangles, the (m)other woman whom Dora adores.
(Appignanesi and Forrester 1992: 147)

In other words, Dora asserted her desire through her symptoms – her cough – and kept it hidden from the therapist's consciousness, but her walking out was a way of achieving independence of the abusing male standing in for an abusing father. If, as Lacan suggested, the hysteric is asking the question: 'Am I a man or a woman?' the therapist can expect to be confused. The way to independence would have possibly been through therapy and through finding an answer to the question rather than by circumventing it. As it was, the possibility of arriving at the truth of her feelings and desires remained only a possibility. In such a case, of course, we now have the benefit of hindsight and of all the work that has been done since. At least now, we can expect that someone who seems to be concealing his or her sexuality by flaunting it will set up a relationship with the therapist where someone is tending to be abusive and someone is abused. A sudden ending can be anticipated and the possibility can be addressed consciously.

The obsessional patient

The opposite difficulty arises with the patient who is obsessional. Such patients are likely to make therapy into a ritual which cannot end. The question being asked by the obsessional patient is: Am I alive or dead? He or she is trapped within deadly repetition that is felt to be safe since it prevents change. The obsessional patient, however, may make a sudden ending if the therapist is unable to anticipate the anger that is being hidden by the obsessional symptom. A moderate degree of obsessionality can help the therapy because it will enable the patient to come regularly to sessions and to tolerate the rhythm of the hour and the week. If the obsessional symptom is itself the presenting problem, it may be inaccessible to psychological treatment and may respond best to cognitive/behavioural approaches. The obsession has been developed in order to protect the patient from an awareness that would be extremely painful.

Nemiah (1961) describes a patient who had obsessional thoughts of anxiety about bumping into someone in the street. Nemiah tracked the anxiety down to fear of knocking the person into the road, and was then able to reveal the wish to do so and the hate and anger that

73

lay behind the wish. In that case, the patient was totally dependent on his mother, still living with her at the age of 40 and fearing to go out without her. His obsessions protected him from the knowledge of his aggression and fury with her and his wish to achieve his freedom and to begin to live his own life. The patient was very afraid of this knowledge and had endured an unpleasant state of mind for some time in order to avoid just this recognition. A therapist who gets near to such a revelation is bound to risk the sudden ending which protects the patient and also protects the therapist from the full brunt of the anger that would come his way.

Slamming the door

Patients with narcissistic difficulties in relating are raging internally, often to the point of walking out of therapy. They may be held back by a number of internal factors. The most positive might be the hope that somehow the therapist's containing presence can help to ease the painful compulsion to hate and destroy. The definition that Kernberg gives for the narcissistic personality implies grandiosity and an inordinate need for praise and reassurance. There is a 'curious apparent contradiction between a very inflated concept of themselves and an inordinate need of tribute from others' (1985: 17). He and Kohut (1971) add the idea of sexual perversity as a characteristic quality of these patients, at least in fantasy. All these writers emphasise the idealising of the therapist that may happen because one way of feeling sufficiently loved and admired is to separate out the people who are not responsive from those who are. The therapist must be kept in the admiring role and the others are then despised. Therapists may be tempted to collude with this because it is a welcome change from addressing the negative feelings of other patients. Kohut gave a rationale for staying with the idealising for a while, but sooner or later the disillusionment must begin. This situation is highly unstable and can change into hatred and scorn of the therapist. If this happens there is clearly a risk of a sudden ending.

Kernberg (1985) has set out a very detailed diagnostic framework in which he makes distinctions between narcissistic, hysterical and borderline pathologies. He arrives at a prognosis for each in general terms and discusses what is likely to happen when the syndromes are mixed. He makes clear that in his view not everyone can or should receive therapy. Borderline psychotic and paranoid symptoms particularly benefit from the support of a team working within an agency and are not likely to do well with a therapist working alone in private practice where there is too much scope for paranoid fear and aggression to become unbearable for either the patient or the therapist.

Therapists need to know how to work in such a way that these people might be able to stay and work through to a more balanced and realistic view of the therapist and therefore of other people. Kohut's view that the therapist should use empathy to work with the patient's feelings of need and entitlement rather than to challenge them is well known. Kernberg believed that because rage and frustration is so prominent in these patients, they need to be faced with their destructiveness. For Kernberg, interpretation of defensive behaviour and its purpose was essential technique if the patient was to stay and work.

Mollon (1993) puts forward a model in which he emphasises the role of the father as the essential element that must be brought in for there to be successful work. That of course does not mean that there must be a mention of the actual father or that there must be a male therapist. What is implied is a need for the therapist to use a thinking function so that the patient is not allowed to stay in an unreal world with only the mother. The therapist must bring in other ideas from his separate thinking processes to challenge the patient to move out of his own fantasies and into a dynamic relationship.

Each of these writers is emphasising a different way in which the therapist can contain the rage and the wish to act out sufficiently for the patient to stay long enough for work to be done. The choice of technique will depend on the therapist's own background, training and supervision, and of course on temperament and the way in which personal therapy has made parts of the self available for use. Somehow the patient needs to feel that the therapist has his measure and can cope with him. Any sign of weakness or fear will lead to panic expressed as rage and a walk out, or a refusal to stay within boundaries of time or place. Thus it is probably most important that the therapist is confident with her own model and feels able to do what is possible within it. Comparison of models is fruitless. In any model the therapist should be willing to be changed by the meeting with the patient. If the therapist tries to stick rigidly to a way of working the result is likely to be disaster because the patient may unconsciously infer that there is some sort of internal partner with whom the therapist is communing. The patient is shut out and an explosive situation is created. The patient will derive much more benefit from an ending that arrives when both the therapist and the patient are able to find a way of agreeing that it is good enough.

A therapist needs to consult feelings about a patient's ending with great care. Responses may come from sadistic and retaliatory feelings that are not recognised, at least at first.

> Dr M had been in therapy for five years and had done useful work on her counter-productive patterns of relationship. Her mother was a difficult and demanding woman who nevertheless loved her daughter and was fiercely protective of her. Dr M found it difficult to express feelings face to face and often resorted in the early days to writing letters which the therapist read and brought to the sessions. After five years she had achieved a better relationship with her partner and was able to manage the emotional demands of her work as a doctor. She came twice a week and had reached a point where she was beginning to think about ending. Dr M found herself quite unable to raise the idea of ending with her therapist. Eventually she wrote a letter in which she said that she would need some help with it because it would be very difficult, but she thought that she was beginning to be ready to look at the possibility of ending. The therapist's response was to be disappointed that the patient could not say these things face to face and had reverted to letter writing which she had not done for some time.
>
> In the next session, the therapist said she had read the letter and understood that the patient wanted some help to fix a date for ending, and perhaps the best time would be the therapist's summer holiday. The patient seemed to accept this and went away. She came back to the next session, burst into tears and said that she had not been able to say how upset she was that the therapist had jumped to the conclusion that she wanted to settle the ending date so soon. She had been afraid to mention ending at all face to face and could see that this related to the kind of response she might have found in her mother. The therapist's response had played right into the fear that her mother's love was conditional and would be taken away if she showed any sign of independence. The therapist searched her own feelings and realised that she had been angry about the move towards independence. She enjoyed

working with this patient and did not want her to go. The response was in effect saying, 'all right, if you want to go, go; see if I care.' After this work had been done, there was a possibility of both working towards an ending and setting an ending date with, perhaps, more regret on the side of the therapist. This was the therapist's problem and while sadness at ending can always be acknowledged, the therapist must be responsible for managing his or her own feelings enough to work without burdening the patient.

Whatever the therapist thinks about the patient's unilateral decision to end, at the last minute he must give his blessing to the one who is departing. This is movingly described by Dorothy Hamilton. She told her supervisor that she was losing a patient. 'He said "Give her your blessing" and just in time I did' (1997: 173).

Silence

Many of the patients who leave therapy prematurely, in the therapist's view, do so because they have not formed a strong attachment to the therapist or, in other words, they have not been able to bring the re-enactment of past conflicts powerfully into the present with the therapist, or the conflicts themselves were buried before they ever surfaced. This is the problem of the schizoid personality, the person who guards against relating most carefully because loving is felt to be more dangerous than indifference. Guntripp (1968) described vividly the arid desert landscape of the schizoid personality. These are people who come to therapy because their lives are empty or dull. They are only half alive and yet they know that there must be more to life. They provide a great challenge to the therapist and are most likely to leave disappointed though quite calm after two or three years of therapy, saying that it was quite interesting but not enough happened. They may not have been literally silent but their speech has been empty.

Of course such patients are doing their best to make sure that nothing *does* happen, but they may also be with a therapist whose personality is not useful to them. Two schizoid people together may never make sparks or be able to stir up some life. In such cases, more interpretation may only increase the intellectualisation and the desert is not allowed to bloom. Jeremy Holmes (1997) has pointed out the problems that may arise for the patient who is avoidant in relationships if he is with a therapist who emphasises the structure and boundaries of the therapy rather than emotional attunement. Such a patient may end too soon. If the patient is ambivalent in relationships he may cling to attachment figures, and if the therapist is too empathic and not sufficiently aware of the need for limits, the patient may stay too long. There are many variations on this theme of patient–therapist fit, but each therapist needs to discover what is her own tendency so that it may adapt to the needs of a particular patient.

Finally, some patients simply leave therapy in silence, giving the therapist no explanation for their disappearance. This may arise from fear, happening just when there is a possibility of greater vulnerability for some reason, but the effect on the therapist is such as to lead to the suspicion that there is unexpressed anger. Most therapists when left in this way feel injured, abandoned, mystified, undervalued. Leaving behind such feelings as these makes the aborted therapy feel like a bereavement or, worse still, a suicide. The silence of the grave is absolute and so very often is an aborted therapy. Therapists have to be able to deal with the feelings aroused in themselves and to try to learn what they can from the experience. Very often, something can be discovered about what was not said or done in time, but sometimes there is no answer, and the therapist has to live with the silence and the sense of failure and whatever that means to him or her personally. One of the reasons for undertaking this profession is, I suspect, that therapists desire to learn to cope with loss, since it is our constant professional experience. However patients leave us, we have to put up with the loss of what had at least the potential to become an intimate relationship.

References

Appignanesi, L. and Forrester, J. (1992) *Freud's Women*, London: Weidenfeld & Nicolson.

Dinnage, R. (1988) *One to One*, Harmondsworth: Penguin.

Freud, A. (1968) 'Acting out', *International Journal of Psycho-analysis* 49: 165.

Guntripp, H. (1968) *Schizoid Phenomena, Object Relations and the Self*, London: Hogarth.

Hamilton, D. (1997) 'Response to Jeremy Holmes', *British Journal of Psychotherapy* 14: 172.

Holmes, J. (1997) 'Too early, too late: endings in psychotherapy – an attachment perspective', *British Journal of Psychotherapy* 14: 159.

Kernberg, O. (1974) 'Further contributions to the study of narcissistic personalities', *International Journal of Psycho-analysis* 15: 215.

Kernberg, O. (1985) *Borderline Conditions and Pathological Narcissism*, London: Aronson.

Klein, M. (1957) 'Envy and gratitude', in (1984) *Envy and Gratitude*, London: Hogarth Press.

Kohut, H. (1971) *The Analysis of the Self*, New York: International Universities Press.

Kohut, H. (1977) *The Restoration of the Self*, New York: International Universities Press.

Mollon, P. (1993) *The Fragile Self*, London: Whurr.

Murdin, L. (1995) 'What harm can it do?', *Psychodynamic Counselling* 1: 3.

Nemiah, J. (1961) *Foundations of Psychopathology*, New York: Oxford University Press.

Philips, A. (1986) *Winnicott*, London: Fontana.

Ragland, E. (1995) *Essays on the Pleasures of Death*, London: Rebus Press.

Samuels, A. (1999) 'From sexual misconduct to social justice', in Mann, D. (ed.) *Erotic Transference and Counter Transference*, London: Routledge.

Symington, N. (1986) *The Analytic Experience*, London: Free Association Books.

Symington, N. (1993) *Narcissism, a New Theory*, London: Karnac.

Sulloway, F. (1992) *Freud Biologist of the Mind*, London: Harvard University Press.

Winnicott, D. W. (1986) 'Fear of breakdown', in Kohon, G. (ed.) *The Independent Tradition*, London: Free Association Books.

5

TIME TO GO

The therapist ends

Since there's no help, come let us kiss and part.
Nay I am done, you get no more of me,
And I am glad, yea glad with all my heart
That thus so cleanly I myself can free.

(Drayton 1975)

Therapists do not generally initiate endings in therapy unless they have very good reason to do so. There are times when people leave because the therapist unconsciously wishes them to do so, but by and large, therapists would prefer patients to stay until there can be a mutual agreement that the patient is ready to go. There are three main identifiable areas in which the therapist may be the one who initiates the ending. The first is obvious. Therapists are susceptible to external reality just as their patients are. They will have partners who need to change jobs, and parents who need looking after. They will get sick and they will die. They may just want to stop practising therapy and retire to the country to open a restaurant or a shop or do the garden. Another group of endings will be those that take place because the therapist cannot or does not wish to continue working with a given patient. Finally there will be the endings that are more or less mutually agreed but have been initiated by the therapist for therapeutic reasons.

The therapist's need

The first group of endings will be likely to be difficult for all sorts of reasons. If the contract had not stated that there would be an ending at a particular time (see Chapter 9), the patient will at best have mixed feelings on being told that the therapist will not continue the work beyond a certain date. Schachter (1992) states that a study of endings shows that as few as 50 per cent of analysands continue to a mutually agreed ending, but the therapist who decrees an ending is rare. When the therapist does have to announce that the work will end at a certain time, the patient is likely to be faced with conflicting desires. On the one hand, there is the anger and disappointment over being abandoned. For some people that might translate directly into action, such as leaving before being left or demonstrating independence by being late for sessions and so on. Depression as a result of powerlessness leading to suppressed anger for sessions and displaced grief might well be expected.

On the other hand, some people work as hard as possible in the time that remains in order to achieve all that can be done in the time available. On the positive side is the wish to end well with the therapist so that he or she can be taken away in the patient's head as a good, conscious image to be called upon when it is needed. This conscious recall of the therapist which is expected and thought about by some people is part of a much deeper need. Unconsciously, there may be the possibility of a sense of self which at this stage is still being formed by multiple experiences in therapy of learning to think and to use what the therapist does and what the therapist is.

The development of a reliable sense of self depends on many factors. First of all, of course, it depends on the definition given to the concept of *self*. The group of people who have a very undeveloped sense of self and cannot reflect usefully on themselves are often described as borderline because they cannot easily process their thoughts and feelings, if at all, and are on the edge of losing control completely. Freud gave the ego the highest position in the psyche as the agency of thinking, rationality and the relationship to the outside world. The self psychologists, most notably Kohut (1977), postulated a self that exists in addition to the psychic structure of id, ego and superego, and is in fact a superordinate structure in its own right. Therapeutically, Kohut's views have been influential because he has emphasised the role of the therapist as a self object; that is, someone who is used by the patient to enable the self-concept to form adequately. The self object is someone who is not wholly you and not wholly me. In Kohut's view, it functions through the therapist's empathy and depends on the therapist being reliable and more loved than hated. The patient may be aware of this need at some level and this need conflicts with and limits the desire to act out resentment and anger.

The essence of Kohut's view of the therapist is that he is valuable to the patient, particularly the narcissistic aspects of the patient, by becoming a self object. This is important because the narcissistic problem has, at its heart, fear of injury from others. As long as the patient fears that closeness to others is going to result in damage to the illusion of omnipotent control by which the other can be kept as nothing more than a mirror image of the self, there is no hope of adequate relationships with others. The therapist is therefore of value because he or she is empathic and does not offer unbearable injuries. This usually means keeping interpretation or response of any kind to a level that conveys understanding and warmth but does not emphasise separateness by over-clever interpretation.

Therapists have disagreed about the extent to which interpretation, in the sense of making links with the past or outside world or commenting on the workings of the psyche, will be useful to these patients. Few would disagree that reliability and a steady technique are of great importance because when the therapist is under great pressure, there is most temptation to retaliate by abandoning the patient. Clearly, therefore, the therapist's decision to end therapy because of illness or other circumstances is likely to feel like an injury. The illusion of unity and control is shattered. One would expect this to cause serious disturbance or at least further regression. In some cases it does, but for many, provided that there is a long enough period of warning, useful work is done under the pressure of time.

Therapists are becoming aware of the need to provide for patients in the event of their own death or serious illness. Therapeutic wills are now generally recognised as a necessity. Another therapist is named as the executor who will be told by the next of kin to speak to the affected patients and will try to see them or decide whether they need a referral to another therapist.The death of a therapist is a blow which may cause a grief reaction, frozen in the regressed infantile state in which thinking capacity had been temporarily delegated to the therapist who is no longer there to help.

Not dying but leaving is a more common trauma imposed by therapists on their patients. I have had the experience of deciding to close a practice in one part of the country in order to move to another area for personal reasons. This meant that I gave those patients who were in psychoanalytic therapy with me one year's notice of my departure. For most people the one year's notice gave time to move through variations of love and hate and to arrive at some sort of readiness to end. A few went to other therapists. Most managed to find resources in themselves both to make extra use of the time that was available and to forgive me enough to let me be at least an ambivalently loved and hated object, rather than all bad.

One patient who found the ending particularly difficult was Mr N. He was an artist but had ceased to paint and did some part-time teaching. He suffered a great deal from bisexual desires and sometimes went to act out his homosexual feelings in men's toilets and clubs. He was married and had one child and once, when his wife was away, he had gone out and left a tap running which had caused a flood. Agonies of guilt and terror had haunted him ever since, along with a sort of awe at the power of his own desire, as he saw it, to cause such a disaster. He had been to various therapists who had tried to cure him of his guilt but he had successfully resisted all attempts to change him.

Twice Mr N left to take up teaching jobs which took him away from therapy, but each time he came back after a few months and returned to therapy. The third time, he resolved to stop running away and to stay until he was cured, which would mean that he would be able to paint again and stay settled in one place with his family. I then told him that I was going to be leaving in a year. He was in the middle of working out the ways in which his outbursts of anger at this wife were expressions of the anger and resentment left over from his infantile and Oedipal experience. His father had left home when he was 4 years old and his mother had withdrawn into a cold, grudging depression. He found me cold, heartless and indifferent, but as long as he was able to continue to see me three times a week, this was bearable for both of us. As soon as he knew that the time was limited, the sense of sin hit him powerfully. My leaving was because he was so evil that I could not bear to stay. He veered wildly between begging forgiveness to the extent of being willing even to say that the therapy had been useful, and a cold rage that expressed itself in arriving late and missing sessions without warning or explanation.

The need for a self object that would enable Mr N to develop a sense of independent self was intense. He longed for a father who would be strong and reliable, but who would also judge him with justice. He had no such reliable and authoritative internal father and I was worried too that he would not be able to make enough use of me in the time remaining to allow him to develop what he needed inside himself. I was especially worried that my leaving would deprive him of the ability to see me as good enough. Mr N's visions of what life might be after I left were split. On the one hand, he might allow himself to be better, having enough inner calm and strength to stay with his wife and not go out looking for men. The trouble with this was partly that such a vision for him at that time meant something static but pure like being in heaven. The other possibility was that he might be taken over by his evil desires, as he saw them, which would take him away from the benevolent father for ever but, as in hell, the picture would be full of his vigorous sexual energy. He was afraid of my judgement of him and his judgement of me. Paintings of the Last Judgement show God the Father enthroned, presiding over the work of the angels and devils who are literally weighing the souls of the dead to determine whether they go to heaven or hell. Heaven has beautiful colours and light but tends to be static. Everyone sits still with beatific expressions. Hell is full of overwhelming action and energy all directed towards torture.

One of his dreams soon after I told him of my impending departure illustrates his anxiety about having or not having what he longed for. He was in a sweet-shop with a very high counter but he was afraid to go up close and look at the sweets. He wanted something that he had once had before but could not remember its name. Perhaps it was some sort of medicinal mixture. He thought to himself, 'Oh it won't be there anyway.' Telling me about it afterwards he said, 'I forgot that I could have mixed it for myself from the other sweets that were there. I was ashamed to go near and ask for something. I was ashamed of the excitement of maybe getting what I wanted. It would have to be offered to me. But then I think I would not have wanted that either. I would have to get it for myself but there is not time. The shop is going to close.'

The thought of ending was bringing him both hope and fear of change. The unconscious conflict between the two was well represented in the sweet-shop dream. On the one hand, he hoped for heaven: milk, honey, medicinal sweets. He wanted to return to his mother's body and have his father's love and approval all at the same time. On the other hand, moving forward brings the risk that he might steal the sweets, or at least be exposed as wanting too much. He might just steal the sweets and run. Mother and father will never give him everything he wants. The fear of ending, like the fear of death, becomes the fear of change itself and what that might mean, and also fear of the loss of the ability to change. If the shop closed or the therapy ended there would no longer be any possibility that some sweets might be offered legitimately, or that he might allow himself to mix them.

Many times Mr N had said that he would be able to paint only after he left me. At the time, I thought that he needed to leave me as the clinging depressed mother who did not want him to grow up and leave her. He could not leave his mother and he could not satisfy what she wanted. If he tried to satisfy her, the powerful image of his father threatened him with punishment and impotence. The only way he could get something for himself was by stealing it. He had been able to feel that he could steal from me in some ways, by taking what I said or did and not letting me know that it was any use to him, but once I said that I would be leaving, I had stolen his time away from him and left him nowhere to go.

Abandonment can feel like deprivation. Mr N had been abandoned by his father and left emotionally alone by his mother. My abandoning him always felt bad at the ends of sessions. The abandonment of ending seemed unforgivable. Yet the therapy itself had perpetuated something of what paralysed him. He was always hoping that I would be the father who would empower him, but he found me frightening and dangerous. He wanted me to be the loving mother who would want him there and yet would free him to be himself. He had become stuck between his conflicting needs, making very little progress because taking in my words made me seem too powerful. In the ending period though, he knew that he would have to move on. Things could not stay the same.

The one way in which Mr N believed that he could feel less impotent was in choosing the time of ending. He wished to leave before I left. He developed the idea that doing so would be a creative and freeing act. I was

85

uncertain whether he needed to do so in reality or whether it would be sufficient for him to know that he could. I continued to say to him that I believed he could derive strength only from destroying me as the mother who deprived him and as the father who would not help him to be a man in his own right, but that perhaps he could still find some use for the time in discovering whether there was any other way of going. The actual ending was a compromise because he chose to leave two weeks before the date that I had proposed, but in this way he gave himself most of the time available.

Once this ending was agreed, a great deal emerged in the last few sessions of his need and love for his mother and his gratitude for my having not let him go too easily, while not holding on to him too powerfully. He was able to tell me that he loved both his father and his mother as well as being furiously angry with them and wanting to wipe them out by flood or fire. This represented the best that he could manage in his feelings about me. His feelings for his wife had become more calm and seemed less to be a matter of projection. Nevertheless, he left me with the feeling that there was much more to do. I experienced a great deal of regret and concern for him. I could not say that there was a resolution of the process by which I had represented the parents, but that there was perhaps a better solution within it. The ending became the ending of therapy, but not the end of the process.

The therapist loses faith

Mr N's ending demonstrated both the difficulty and pain of an imposed ending and also its possible value. A second group of endings is even more difficult for both patient and therapist to tolerate. These are the endings caused by the therapist ceasing to have the heart or the courage to continue. These sorts of endings occur for a variety of reasons. We hear about them often because they lead to complaints. Ethical questions are raised by the patient who is hurt, feels damaged and wishes to force the therapist to continue against his or her will. In fantasy, the patient believes that he can compel the therapist to want him after all. The therapist's wish to end is all a terrible mistake. One or two examples have come to light where the patient has developed a severe version of what Balint (1968) calls a malignant regression.

Balint describes the situation in which a patient cannot bear the usual frustrations of the therapeutic situation in which, essentially, the therapist gives only words:

> traditional behaviour of sympathetic but passive objectivity is felt by certain patients as unwarranted and unbearable frustration.

As a result, he

> decides – either for himself or in agreement with his patient – that a new regime must be established by doing something more, over and above the traditional passivity. This something more amounts always to gratifying some of his patient's regressive urges, to responding positively to the patient's acting out. As a rule this change brings some immediate improvement.
>
> (Balint 1968: 113)

Unfortunately, as Balint goes on to point out, this gradual approach to gratifying the patient leads to greater and greater demands. As he puts it, the patient responds gratefully with the more developed part of himself, but the seriously regressed part just demands further gratification to prove the therapist's love. The problem is intensified because the patient's need is such that the gratification must be irrespective of the patient's co-operation or gratitude, and must be offered without any taint of compulsion. Any frustration provokes a vehement response and further acting out.

Most therapists come across the kind of difficult regression that Balint is talking about at some point either directly or through the difficulties of a colleague. The patient will be persistent far beyond the norm in demanding extra time or physical contact. There will be telephone calls, extra sessions, difficulties in ending sessions on time. The therapist will often try to find reasons to accede to the demands in the beginning. As Balint points out, this may bring a period of calm and is such a relief that there is a strong temptation to continue in that direction. Theoretical justification could be found in the concept of management or Winnicott's *nursing care* (1985: 131). Intuition is often invoked: 'I just know that he needs this or that in reality and symbolic care will not be enough.' Nothing is ever enough, and sooner or later there will be a point beyond which the therapist is not prepared to go. The telephone calls will come in the night or will break too often into personal time and will lead to objections from other family members. In desperation, the therapist makes a sudden move to end, either by trying to make a referral to a more senior colleague or simply by trying to hand over to the medical or psychiatric services. Sometimes a specific referral provides continuity that helps with the ending. Sometimes a referral to a specific person emphasises too much the continuing emotional presence of the original therapist and therefore the difficulty. Anne Leigh has written about termination and referral issues for counsellors. She discusses referral letters and offers a prescription for making a good referral (1998).

Ferenczi's experiments in treating regression by gratification were not encouraging. In some cases there was a small improvement, in some the result was disastrous (Balint 1968: 113). Nevertheless, Ferenczi died leaving many questions unanswered and we certainly cannot say that his methods would never have been successful. Balint pursues the idea that a regression may lead the patient to make demands for satisfactions that belong to very early infantile states. He points out that to gratify these needs may be a different category of behaviour from gratifying demands which have become genital. The difference is expressed in terms of the type of regression: is the patient seeking to make use of the therapist with the regression in the service of a new beginning, or is he aiming only at gratification from the other person? This question is obviously difficult to answer. Difficulties arise because so often it can be answered only once the patient is already in the midst of the work.

Balint recommends that the therapist should consider some forms of regression to be helpful and potentially in the service of development. This is currently a common view of regression, but there is still no infallible answer to the question of how to deal with the patient whose demands are for gratification only. Perhaps in many cases there is no alternative to an ending which is just made as tolerable as it can be for both parties. Balint, however, does have some hope. He illustrates his position with a description of a patient who asked for an extra session over a weekend. In this case the therapy was just entering the stage where it might become a malignant regression:

> What I tried to do in this case was first to recognise and respond to his distress so that he should feel that I was

with him and then to admit that I did not feel that an extra
session granted by me would be powerful enough to give
him what he expected and perhaps even needed at this
moment; in addition this would make him small and weak
while his analyst would become great and powerful, which
was not desirable. For all these reasons the request was not
granted. The patient then departed dissatisfied.

(Balint 1968: 171)

Balint's patient was dissatisfied, but he returned and was able to
work with what had been said to him. Searles (1965) demonstrates
the need to work with his own sexual tension. He tells of the attraction he felt to a woman patient and his attempt to deny it by speaking
to her of the maternal transference in terms of feeding and her need
for him to feed her adequately. But, he points out, the patient was
well aware of his feelings of sexual desire for her. She seems to
have pointed it out tolerantly and gently. Some patients are not so
kind and are capable of abusing the therapist in revenge for their
own unfulfilled and unspoken longings. When there is a powerful
erotic desire on either side, the therapist is likely to be tempted into
a precipitous ending out of fear, rather than for the benefit of the
patient.

One parent alone with a child runs the risk of potentially abusive
power. Internally, at least, the therapeutic relationship needs the
reflective third, whether an actual supervisor or an internalised therapist or a supervisor from the past. Sadly, this is not always enough.
For some therapeutic pairs, the only answer seems to be an ending.
The therapist may find the demands of the very regressed patient
too much to handle. The work with Mrs Q shows how difficult it
can be to continue to work in these circumstances:

Mrs Q is a recently divorced woman in her late twenties.
She is a teacher working with adolescents and presents
herself as bright and sharp. She comes to a therapist after
having interviewed three other therapists in the area, all of
whom she had rejected because they were not prepared
to see her after school hours for a reduced fee. She settled
on her actual therapist, Mrs R, with a bad grace, complaining that she needed more empathy with the difficulties
she had experienced with the previously visited therapists.
At some level she probably knew that she needed some
toughness in the therapist. As a result, the therapy began

with a clearly negative feeling. The therapist was just tolerated. Mrs R tried interpreting the scorn that she experienced as Mrs Q's way of protecting herself from having to feel any gratitude for finding someone who actually would take her on for a low fee at the desired time of day. Mrs R had taken her on because, in spite of some misgivings, she saw a possibility of working with the narcissistic problems presented – the failed marriage and a powerfully negative relationship with the headteacher who was an older woman – and also because she had a space at the time requested.

The first sessions were very bumpy. The patient became extremely angry because Mrs R was not being sufficiently empathic and because her use of words was irritating. On one occasion, she was being told about the patient's desire to move out of her shared flat. Mrs R said, 'You are cramped in your present home.' The patient became enraged. 'I can't stand people who say "home". Why can't you say "house"?' Very little was known about the patient's history except that Mrs Q's mother was ill and in hospital a great deal during her childhood and her father had left and remarried when the patient was 10 years old. Any mention of the past was felt to be an avoidance on the therapist's part of her responsibility in the present and for not being sufficiently understanding, wise and helpful.

At the same time, the patient was doing all in her power to prevent the therapist from being able to understand what she was saying. The patient's communications were always rapid and confusing, with stories beginning in the middle and referring to people who had not been previously mentioned, but giving a clear indication that they should be known to the therapist already. 'You remember I told you about Joy . . .'

A great deal of the scorn was related to the therapist's having a different style from the two male therapists who had been interviewed by the patient. Mrs R interpreted this as the scorn for the therapist who *would* take her on, like the mother who remained, in contrast with the ones who had not been willing to make the necessary concessions. Interpretations were greeted with rage and comments about the stupidity of the therapist. 'You just want to make it all my fault so that you don't have to see how you're not

THE THERAPIST ENDS

helping me.' The therapist acknowledged that she was not helping much but said quietly that perhaps there would have to be some attention to why the patient found it so difficult to see anything at all as helpful. At the end of the third session, the patient said, 'I'm not leaving until you say something useful.' The therapist was quietly firm and Mrs Q left after five minutes. The next time she found reasons to stay even longer, and the therapist became anxious that she would intrude into the next patient's time.

Supervision was helpful in containing the therapist's anxiety. Various techniques were employed to make the end of the session less difficult. There was a temporary improvement, but in the sixth session the therapist told the patient about her impending holiday which was a month away. The patient stayed, refusing to move until the therapist said that she was going to collect the next patient. Mrs Q then rushed out of the building and stood screaming outside the therapist's window until the receptionist persuaded her to leave. The therapist decided that she could not cope with such upset to her other patients and wrote to say that she would not see Mrs Q any more but would help her to find another therapist if she wished. Mrs Q wrote to the therapist's professional body to complain about Mrs R as incompetent for having abandoned her in the middle of ongoing work. The complaint was not upheld because Mrs Q had constantly told the agency that the therapy was harmful to her, and the conclusion reached was that she could not claim that a referral elsewhere was potentially more damaging, and in fact, such a referral might actually help.

From the outside, it is very difficult to see how this therapist could have worked more helpfully within this situation. There is probably a sense in which the problem is one of personality. There are some therapists with an internal warmth and authority which comes across to patients in a way that leaves no need for dangerous acting out. As in teaching, this seems to be difficult to acquire. Either you have it or you do not. Sometimes, a crisis of this sort will produce it, but, as with classroom teaching, the therapist who is tentative or anxious at the first time of challenge is unlikely to be able to regain the necessary authority. The patient at some level knows that the therapist is powerless to prevent the kind of scene that happened in this case, and is of course, at one level, setting out to destroy the therapy. Whether any therapist could have worked usefully with this patient is debatable. Certainly, the implication is that the therapy as it developed was too dangerous and had to be stopped. The therapist did not address the difficulty and fear for the patient in being alone with a woman who represented her mother and symbolically was felt to have abandoned her and also somehow deprived her of her father. Perhaps it was just too dangerous with this particular therapist if she could not hold the damaging part of the patient sufficiently firmly and safely.

Anna Freud (1968) makes a useful distinction between the habitual acting out of the impulsive patient, and the neurotic patient who acts out in order to communicate with the therapist. She characterised the impulsive patients as those who are psychotic, pre-psychotic, paranoid or addictive. These groups will act impulsively whether or not they are in therapy and will not restrict their actions to the therapeutic context, however carefully the therapist works. To work with these sorts of difficulties implies accepting the inevitability of destructive behaviour of various sorts and the willingness to tolerate a certain amount of it while knowing very clearly where one's limits must be set. Nevertheless, she points out that even in these cases, memories, or as we might prefer to say today, meaning, can be extracted from observing and experiencing the behaviours. It is therefore possible that some sorts and degrees of these behaviours can be brought sufficiently into the therapy and contained there for the work of symbolising and reflecting to be done. This will depend on the tolerance and firmness of the therapist, although Anna Freud herself places the responsibility for the safety of the therapy on the ego strength of the patient:

> There is no doubt of course that also in this extended form of acting out the patient repeats his past and that memory can be extracted from the re-enactment. Whether the ensuing reconstructions serve the recovery of the patient will depend in the last resort not on the quantity or quality of the acting out itself but on the intactness or otherwise of the ego's synthetic function to which the regained material is submitted.
>
> (1968: 169)

If the therapist could survive and contain the anxiety, he could say to the patient that it would be a great pity if the disastrous experiences of the past had to be repeated to the extent of ending the therapy. This may well be heard as a threat which, of course, to some extent it is. On the other hand, it may provide a patient with a way out of the impasse if the therapist is able to show that he or she is nearly at the point of giving up but is still prepared to go on working if the patient will allow. The only hope in this sort of difficulty is to address the patient's thinking potential and to combine it with very firm management.

Referral in a hopeless situation

Masud Khan (1989) gives an account of a therapy in which he worked with a patient who had driven her first therapist, whom she called Calamity, to the point of abandonment. She had, however, managed to make a referral to Masud Khan before she gave up completely. Masud Khan began work with the patient with the advantage of already knowing the sort of uproar that she created. He describes the first meeting in which he made clear that his houseboy was available in the background to deal with any trouble. He also shook the patient's hand with a powerful grip, shocking her by his strength and his willingness to demonstrate it to her. He tells us that he then had no problem with her in the sense that, although the therapeutic work was difficult, the acting out in the sessions was minimal. One conclusion we can draw from this is that although physical strength and reinforcements are desirable in this sort of case, there is also some help to be had in knowing what has gone before and facing the patient very clearly with the destructive nature of their behaviour. If this can be done, it may be possible to avoid the disastrous ending even without Masud Khan's physique or domestic retinue. What Khan's demonstration of strength does reveal is the importance sometimes for the patient of knowing that the therapist will not change in terms of the firmness of the management and the framework of the therapy. At the same time, he shows that he is willing to listen and be changed internally.

Ending an impasse

In cases where the therapist decides that the therapy cannot be improved, it may be ended gradually and by design rather than catastrophically. Freud ended the analysis with the Wolf Man, not because he could not continue but because he was aware that no progress was being made. He had set out the course which he

93

considered an analysis must take if it were to be considered complete. First of all the infantile phantasies must be laid bare. By this he meant that beneath symptoms, whether phobic, hysterical, or obsessional, there will be phantasies which are derived from infantile misunderstandings of adult sexuality and the bodily functions of the child. These phantasies must be discovered from the symptom itself and from clues such as dreams and details of the person's history as it is remembered in snatches and fragments. Once these have been put together, there is the possibility of moving on to something else:

> After the infantile phantasies had been disposed of in this way, it would be possible to begin a second portion of the treatment which would be concerned with the patient's real life.
>
> (Freud 1918: 283)

In other words, the turning away from reality which the symptom allows in the present will be understood in the context of an infantile phantasy. If this understanding is not used by the patient, however, the normal process of analysis will come to a standstill. Freud found the Wolf Man to be resistant in a way that will be familiar to most therapists. He had an attitude of 'obliging apathy'. He listened, he understood and he remained unapproachable. He had an unimpeachable intelligence and understood everything that was said to him perfectly, but he remained largely unaffected. In fact, Freud says that when there was some small change, this caused him to take fright to such an extent that he ceased to work altogether. Freud understood that there was an attachment to him, but saw it only as a counterbalance to the fear of independence. In fact, it seems as though the love for the analyst might well prevent the patient from wishing to get better. In any case, a firm determination to end seems to have galvanised the Wolf Man into further work because the alternative would have been to leave without either his loved analyst or the change that might help him to survive alone.

Freud found by decreeing that the analysis would end on a certain date, that the patient was able to set to work and produce more useful associations in the remaining time. Even though the analysis was ended firmly by Freud, the patient still had further work to do, and although the neurotic symptoms improved, there was a need for the patient to return to analysis later with Ruth Mack Brunswick

(Murdin 1994: 357). Nevertheless, there is sometimes a clear rationale for the therapist to end the work, either because he cannot find a way to make progress and therefore the patient is wasting time and money, or because the therapist judges that an ending date will lead to better progress.

However good the rationale, therapists are taking a risk if they decide to impose or even suggest an ending date. Klauber (1986) was against imposing an ending. He writes of two patients who found ending difficult. Both had suffered loss and were unable to deal with it and return to healthy functioning. Both formed a strong attachment to Klauber and were unable to recognise any negative feelings towards him. One of them, Mrs P, was the more psychotic of the two and she, ironically, had been referred to him with a flying phobia. She proved quite unable to fly or leave. After five years of five-times-weekly sessions, Klauber felt that the analysis was stuck and suggested that she consult a colleague of his. She did so but was not willing to transfer to the colleague. She continued in analysis with Klauber at decreasing frequency of sessions and he was able to say that the analysis achieved 'some success'. Working with her led to a constant confusion and anxiety in the analyst, yet Klauber points out that paradoxically the analyst usually wants to keep such patients because of the power of the libidinal connection between them, however negative that might be. He concludes, like de Simone (1997), that analysts should not end analysis but should wait until the patient is ready. Anything else leads to trauma for the patient and possibly for the analyst too.

Klauber makes the vital point that the therapist must suffer the illness of the patient but that the therapist must get better first. This is an immensely important aspect of analytic therapy. The therapist must certainly make every effort to understand and overcome the difficulties that the patient inevitably imposes on him or her as a communication of the problem. The therapist must use his or her own therapy and supervision or consultation to the utmost. A cardinal virtue needed for this work is patience. Nevertheless, there are times when an ending is indicated and may be the only way in which the therapist can recover from the spell cast by the patient. If reasonable notice is given, the patient may well be able to use the therapist's recovery to good advantage, provided that the therapist is genuinely not being sadistic, careless or impatient but has taken every step to ensure that the process is responsible and in the patient's best interests.

References

Balint, M. (1968) *The Basic Fault*, London: Tavistock.

de Simone, G. (1997) *Ending Analysis*, London: Karnac.

Drayton, M., (1975) in Gardner, H. (ed.) *Oxford Book of English Verse*, Oxford: Oxford University Press.

Freud, Anna (1968) 'Acting out', *International Journal of Psycho-analysis* 79: 165.

Freud, S. (1918) 'From the history of an infantile neurosis', *SE* 17.

Khan, Masud (1989) 'The empty headed', in *Hidden Selves*, London: Maresfield.

Klauber, J. (1986) *Difficulties in the Analytic Encounter*, London: Free Association Books. (Originally published 1981.)

Kohut, H. (1977) *The Restoration of the Self*, New York: International Universities Press.

Leigh, A. (1998) *Referral and Termination Issues for Counsellors*, London: Sage.

Murdin, L. (1994) 'Time to go – therapist induced endings in psychotherapy', *British Journal of Psychotherapy* 10 (3).

Schacter, J. (1992) 'Concepts of termination and post termination in patient–analyst contact', *International Journal of Psycho-analysis* 73 (1).

Searles, H. (1965) *Collected Papers on Schizophrenia*, London: Maresfield.

Winnicott, D. W. (1985) *The Maturational Processes and the Facilitating Environment*, London: Hogarth.

6

WHAT IS TRUTH?

Values and valuing endings

As soon as I ask the question 'when *should* a therapy end?' I am in the realm of values. The ending very often occurs as a consensus when the values of patient and therapist coincide sufficiently. When there is conflict, whether hidden or overt, the therapist must consult his value system as well as his intellect. In this, as in all that we do, the therapist is limited with knowing only her own conscious part in what happens. The analytic therapist does her best to listen to the patient and to allow for her own unconscious. In Chapter 1, I considered the way in which the theoretical model might determine the therapist's image of a good ending. In addition, the therapist's conscious attitude will be formed by personal values and by personal moral development. There are also some professional values which might achieve a consensus: all therapists, for example, share a concern for truth.

Each therapist attaches meaning to the words *values*, *morals* and *ethics* and each area will be relevant in the ending process. This chapter will deal with the broad issues of the underlying values that will enter into the therapist's decision to end and the conduct of the ending phase. This will involve a consideration of underlying goals which may not be consciously formulated for therapists and patients. Chapter 7 will look at the ethical principles and codes that govern the process of therapy for individuals and the profession as a whole. Ethics and the science of ethics has a public implication. Morality is usually defined as the personal value system that sets out the distinction between right and wrong or good and evil. A discussion of the values underlying the ending process will inevitably also have to address the way in which the therapist makes use of his or her values in choosing how to apply theory and technique to an individual. In other words, *valuing* in practice may not always accord with stated *values*.

Are there any values that all psychotherapists might accept? This is a difficult question. Positivists would deny that there are any universal truths in the realm of values. 'Goodness', 'rightness', etc. are always relative. Most of the debates within the profession arise from matters of values rather than of fact. The process of seeking to establish agreed national vocational qualifications for psycho-therapy has led to an acceptance of the differences that divide the profession and also to a search for underlying common values. Although some do not accept that psychotherapy can be described in terms of behavioural objectives at all, for those who experimented with such descriptions during the consultation process, there was general agreement that we all seek, and therefore presumably all value:

- a model of the mind and of its functioning
- a model of human development
- a model of change.

None of these models is without controversy. Even if all three are necessary to the practice of psychotherapy, each therapist is likely to emphasise the value of one area more than another. Many therapists are looking for a greater understanding of the patient and for the patient to have achieved this for himself. Lacanians may emphasise living with the emergence of the unconscious, and will devalue rational control as the supreme good. Some models will place greater value on structural change in the mind while others will value the capacity for relationship and interaction.

Valuing development

Therapists look for change. This may be seen in terms of a devel-opmental metaphor. In other words, patients will be seen as having been arrested in their mental development at a point of fixation, and value will be attached to helping them to move beyond this point at least to another stage. A more sophisticated version of this view will be that the patient should be able to achieve a flexible level of functioning which will include and allow for forms of thinking, feeling and behaviour that relate to various phases in the develop-mental metaphor. Another approach to valuing development may be to look for differences in relating. The therapist who values object relations theory will be likely to look particularly for a patient to be able to develop more mature relationships with appropriate dependency and intimacy within the transference relationship or in the therapeutic alliance. Accounts of relationships outside the therapy may be taken as the touchstone for improvement.

Valuing happiness

In developing a value system as a psychotherapist, each individual needs to examine his or her personal moral system which will have been formed by internalisation and identification. These values will be old family and parental injunctions such as 'always be considerate' or 'always be truthful'. As a member of a Western society and culture, I am likely to pay at least lip-service to some of the accepted value words and phrases such as *reason, autonomy, relief of suffering* and *resolution of conflict*. Freedom is also a value that needs to be considered in any discussion of the aims of psychotherapy. Happiness may no longer be widely regarded as an acceptable aim in psychotherapy, although it formed the basis of early nineteenth-century utilitarianism and has occupied an important place in twentieth-century value systems. If we do dispense with happiness we had better be able to justify such a move, as many patients will expect that they are going to find at least a degree of happiness.

Freud made it clear from the beginning that analytic work would not necessarily lead to greater happiness. In 'Beyond the pleasure principle' (1920) he wrote that the organism seeks to reduce the level of excitation or at least keep it stable, making it a special case under Fechner's principle of the tendency towards stability, and equated lowering of excitation with pleasure (German: *lust*). He pointed out that:

> there exists in the mind a strong *tendency* towards the pleasure principle, but that that tendency is opposed by certain other forces or circumstances so that the final outcome cannot always be in harmony with the tendency towards pleasure.
>
> (Freud 1920: 4)

What opposes the working of the pleasure principle which always seeks to discharge any tension or excitation immediately, is the prohibition and demand of what might be called conscience or the part of the ego known as the super ego. This causes most trouble when the commands are not conscious but are operating from hidden depths. The self-preservative and thinking function of the ego may also encourage waiting for gratification or shelving the demands of the pleasure principle while the hidden voices are being obeyed. If the death instinct has any power, it is opposed to any pleasure except stasis. Freud believed that analysis is on the side of life. It should reduce neurotic misery, but he understood that any process which increases the degree of consciousness and the extent of the relationship to reality is bound to lead to much pain and difficulty.

Freud was writing in the context of nineteenth-century thought and was therefore likely to consider the importance of happiness or pleasure. The two words have slightly different connotations in English but both do have definitions that relate to the enjoyment of what is considered to be good or desirable, and the avoidance of pain. *Happiness* is perhaps a broader word than *pleasure*, with more possibility of a spiritual dimension and less emphasis on sensation. Therapists might put other goals first but most patients would rate the increase of happiness and the avoidance of pain as high on the list of their conscious goals. The theory on which most psychotherapy is based accepts that neurotic disturbance is the result of an attempt, either conscious or unconscious, to avoid pain, therefore any therapy that seeks to change the defensive structures must be concerned with the balance of pleasure and pain and must be concerned with altering the way in which the individual deals with pain.

When a prospective patient enters the consulting room, she may therefore be seeking something quite different from the purposes that the therapist may entertain.

> Mrs S comes to see a psychotherapist. She has been referred by her family doctor because he considers that she is suffering from depression but does not wish to take anti-depressants. She is constantly visiting the surgery and complaining of minor ailments. The GP's referral letter sounds irritated and clearly he wishes to have her taken off his hands. When she arrives for an assessment session she is smartly dressed in a suit, with a noticeably short skirt. She plunges straight in: 'I do not want to waste my time or your time and I would like to know whether you can be any help to me. I just needed a little bit of consideration from Dr T, but he is always too busy. I shall not want to be here for a long time. You hear about people who go to a therapist for months or even years. Well, I'm not going to do that. I just want to know what you do so that I can decide whether you can help me.'

Many things willl be passing through a therapist's mind at this point about the way in which this woman relates to people and her businesslike desire to be on top of things. This has a perfectly rational side to it, but also of course there are various other messages which will be interpreted according to the theoretical model of the therapist.

Mrs S continued, when invited, to talk about her past and current situation. She had a job as a publisher's proof-reader which she did not much like as it was 'only reading other people's books'. She had been married for about a year, to a man whom she had known since she was a teenager. She had felt that this marriage was a mistake and that it had limited and confined her. Her husband was not a very powerful man, she said, and she found herself managing everything for both of them. Now she had come to despise him. 'He clings to me. He thinks that just because I married him, I will stay with him. Well, he's wrong. I need my independence. I've heard that therapy helps you to find yourself and take more for yourself. That's what I want. I'm tired of giving so much to him. It was the same with my parents. They were all right I suppose but they always left it to me to have all the ideas and I got fed up with them. I left home when I went to university and I hardly ever go back. They just bore me.'

In response to a question from the therapist about what she hoped to gain from therapy, Mrs S replied, 'I just want to be happy. I suppose I want you to help me to be more selfish.' At this point, the therapist was thinking that there was indeed much work to be done, but that it was along the lines of making Mrs S more aware of her existing self-ishness than of helping her to increase it.

This therapist is therefore confronted by ethical problems in deciding whether to work with this patient and technical questions about how to work if both wish to begin. The situation also raises questions about the divergence of values. At least in the present, the therapist was not able to accept the patient's valuation of the situation and of the use that she wanted to make of therapy. I shall return to this patient later.

Measuring happiness

John Stewart Mill addressed the difficulty of taking happiness or pleasure as an overriding goal in establishing the system of utilitarianism. He put forward the following criterion by which actions could be judged as moral or immoral:

> The creed which accepts as the foundation of morals, Utility, or the Greatest Happiness Principle, holds that actions are right in proportion as they tend to promote happiness, wrong as they tend to produce the reverse of happiness. By happiness is intended pleasure and the absence of pain; by unhappiness, pain and the privation of pleasure.
>
> (Mill 1861)

The utilitarians worked from Jeremy Bentham's view, stated at the opening of his *Principles of Morals and Legislation* (1789): 'Nature has placed man under the governance of two sovereign masters, pain and pleasure.' All actions are to be judged as useful or not according to the extent to which they augment or diminish the sum of human happiness. Bentham invented the Felicific Calculator which sets out to measure units and increments of happiness. Perhaps if we could agree on how to measure happiness we might be more able to use it as a guide to the patient's goals and therefore to a person's desire to be untroubled by the process of psychotherapy.

Mill, however, did not accept that happiness alone is enough to define the good. He added the view that there are different qualities of happiness to be considered. We might all have moments of happiness in doing something fairly basic like eating an ice-cream or listening to a sentimental song. We might value the ability to enjoy small things but would not elevate these pleasures into a definition of happiness. We might also be aware of more disreputable pleasures that we would not wish to admit to in public and which we would certainly not wish to include in a statement of what constitutes the good. Such a viewpoint implies that there are valid judgements that can be made over which kinds of pleasure or happiness are best. Mill was clear that such judgements are appropriate and can be made by some people better than by others:

> It is better to be a human being dissatisfied than a pig satisfied; better to be Socrates dissatisfied than a fool satisfied

and if the fool or the pig are of a different opinion, it is because they only know their own side of the question. The other party to the comparison knows both sides.

(Mill 1861: Chapter 2)

Socrates would be satisfied only by an offer of happiness that had a high degree of rationality and morality in it. Mill put the point that there is more to the idea of what is good than simple pleasure. He added the view that those with the knowledge of many pleasures and possibilities are in a better position to judge what is good than those who have only very limited horizons.

The psychotherapist has experienced not only his or her own training which usually includes intensive therapy of the sort being practised. The question is whether this gives enough expertise to allow the therapist to decide, for example, in the case of Mrs S, that he has a better idea of what she *ought* to want. There is a difficulty in that if the therapist goes ahead in working towards the goal of greater self-awareness, he may be doing something that the patient does not want and is therefore infringing her freedom of choice and her autonomy. In fact, we would not be surprised if greater self-awareness made her more unhappy at least in the short term and therefore was directly contrary to her consciously expressed wish.

For these sorts of reasons, psychotherapists have generally preferred not to deal in terms of happiness and unhappiness. A more promising field in which to seek the values that we could all accept and hope for patients to attain has been seen in the concept of autonomy. The argument for it is that if we cannot agree on specific goals or outcomes, the best we can offer to our patients is that they should achieve increased autonomy and be able to go away making more use of choice and self-determination. We should in fact be freeing them from any dependence on our views of what the greatest good might be.

Valuing autonomy

Holmes and Lindley (1989) accept Mill's view that happiness is not a sufficient description of the good. Mill's view is that true happiness is that which an individual would choose if his choices were not constrained by irrationality or ignorance. Being autonomous implies being able to choose for oneself what is good. They go on to assert that autonomy is 'an essential part of human well being ... a reasonable level of autonomy should be regarded as important in the same way as basic forms of physical health care, (1989: 65–66). For those who do not have autonomy in this sense, psychotherapy is 'the best and, in many cases, the only remedy' (1989: 66).

If autonomy is a central value, it might help us to assess readiness for ending therapy. We could look at the degree of autonomy achieved. This argument has several flaws in addition to the ones mentioned above. One is stated by Erwin (1997), who argues that autonomy should not be the only or even the primary goal of psychotherapy for several reasons. First, it may not be the patient's goal. He gives an example of a scientist who presents with a problem in sleeping. The scientist does not seek to have increased autonomy but does wish to sleep in order to be able to work. Erwin seems to be implying here that it would be possible to be setting out to increase the autonomy of the patient without at the same time taking note of his own wishes for control of his sleep problem. A response to this requires a discussion of theoretical model and technique.

We would be greatly helped with the difficulties of deciding the goals and the degree of achievement of a patient in therapy if we were able to take the patient's wish as expressed in the presenting problem or at any stage in therapy as the absolute arbiter of decision making. In fact of course, in many cases, the patient does not give the therapist an opportunity to affect the decision. In a majority of cases, however, therapists claim that the decision is a matter of mutual agreement and the therapist's viewpoint has at least some weight. If the therapist does not accept the patient's view because of an underlying judgement, this is likely to have an impact on the patient's decision and the experience of ending. The therapist at least should try to be aware of the processes leading to his or her viewpoint.

If the therapist *can* accept the patient's view, this would appear to solve some of the problems in a democratic and morally acceptable way. On the other hand, it creates great difficulties for anyone working psychoanalytically. In the first place, how can a patient in the early stages of therapy who is wishing to take a flight into health, or just plain flight, be expected to assess the value of continuing with work that will take years and will follow an inherently unpredictable shape? Second, and much more crucially, there are difficulties that arise from the structure of the mind implied by psychoanalytic theory. The theory of repression implies that the conscious part of the mind does not know what is repressed. If a large or significant part of what could be known is not known, how can an individual be free to make responsible and informed choices?

The difficulties of working from the principle of autonomy towards conclusions about what should be done in psychoanalytic work are discussed by Hinshelwood (1997). The model that lies behind the psychoanalytic method of treatment is the medical model, and medical ethics and values are bound to be important whether they are accepted or rejected. Hinshelwood considers the decision-making process and recognises that 'at times in our work we sense that we must proceed in spite of the patient, and this does not bring us – doctor, nurse or psychoanalyst – into the category of torturer or brain-washer (1997: 20). If we accept that there are times when we have to proceed against the conscious wishes of the patient, then we are clearly elevating something else above the value of autonomy. The clinical situation might develop as follows for Mrs S:

Mrs S has been attending therapy for six months. During that time she has talked about her difficulties with her husband. The therapist has continually tried to encourage her to consider the part that she plays in causing him to be as he is. These attempts have been somewhat muted because the patient seems to be always on the verge of leaving and the therapist has decided that it would be best to go slowly and encourage the development of a useful therapeutic alliance before making too much challenge or confrontation.

Mrs S then came to a session telling of a dream in which she was outside a window trying to get into the therapist's room. She could see someone else in the room but could not make herself heard. The therapist interpreted this as her desire to allow herself to be inside the room and therefore inside the therapy instead of hovering about just outside. This of course omitted to deal fully with the guilt over her incestuous wish to come between the therapist and another patient as she might have wished as a child to come between her parents, or, on the other hand, the wish to be outside and to have someone else be the patient. The following week the patient said 'I've decided to leave now. This has helped me to see that I really need to leave and stop bothering about what other people think.

You were wrong about that dream. I don't want to be inside. I just have to act for myself. Do you think that's right?'

The therapist is confronted with the problem of whether or not to accept the patient's conscious wish to leave. There are all sorts of questions to answer here about the possible meaning of the dream and the patient's unconscious messages. For example, why does the patient say she doesn't care about other people's views but then asks the therapist for her view? This paradox needs to be addressed at some point, but a more fundamental question is whether the therapist's values are in conflict to the point where they need to be acknowledged at least internally and perhaps also to the patient. For example, the therapist might be thinking that this patient needs to continue in therapy in order to sort out the conflicts about intimacy that could be seen in the dream and in the patient's views of it. In other words, the therapist might consider the paternalistic position which would be to tell the patient that she thinks that she has more useful work to do and should stay in therapy and struggle with the demands of an intimate relationship. Clearly there is no guarantee that this would be accepted by the patient and it might lead to a hostile ending in which the patient would simply walk out.

The example of Mrs S is certainly one in which there is some ambivalence in the patient which she has shown in her question to the therapist as well as in her dream. The therapist, if following an analytical model, would make at least some attempt to explore the ambivalence rather than simply allow the patient to walk away. The medical model allows the doctor to choose for the patient if the patient is not considered to be in a position to make rational choices for him- or herself. Psychotherapy is in a particularly difficult position here because people come to a therapist for the very reason that the decision-making process in some area has become problematic. The analytic model would say that there is a problem in the patient's mental processes arising from a hitch in a developmental process or an illness in the faculty for remembering and forgetting or a failure to achieve an adequate sense of self and other, or even not being sufficiently in touch with his own unconscious processes. Wherever one places the emphasis, the process of psychotherapy will be designed to change something that will make the patient more capable of thinking in a healthy way. In other words, we are dealing with what has been perhaps the greatest value of Western culture in the twentieth century: rationality.

Valuing rationality within autonomy

There have been endless papers written and debates conducted about whether psychotherapy is a science or an art. Wherever we might decide to place it as a discipline on that spectrum, we cannot escape from the cultural valuation of rationality that has so far survived the postmodernist critique. We deal with the demand that patients should be able to function well rationally as well as emotionally. Disturbance of thought in terms of obsessions, phobias, depression, fear of intimacy, is the basis of the need for psychotherapy and patients will be at various stages of improvement during the work. The therapist will make a judgement, when ending is mentioned, about the position that the patient has reached in relation to the capacity for thought, and this judgement will of course depend on the therapist's own capacity for thought.

A model of the mind that emphasises defence will invite a consideration of splitting and the consequent valuing of wholeness or self-awareness. Splitting as a defence is defined by Kleinians as the ability to avoid pain and conflict by attributing certain thoughts and feelings to an agent other than the conscious self and thus to avoid having to own whatever is expected to be painful. If splitting is operating at a high level, the patient will attribute her own feelings or thoughts to another, possibly to the therapist, and therefore will not be in a position to make a judgement from herself as a whole. The question is whether the patient's decisions are honoured in such circumstances.

To return to Mrs S:

> The therapist replied to Mrs S's question as follows: 'You are perhaps telling me that you have some doubts about me and the therapy but you still want to know what I think, as if you might not be quite sure that you want to leave.' Mrs S then got angry and said, 'You therapists are all the same. You just want people to stay in therapy for ever so that you can have a nice fat income. You're just like him [her husband].' The therapist was taken aback by this attack, but recognised that a process of splitting at this point could perhaps be made conscious. 'I understand that you see both your husband and me as making huge demands on you. If you see me as just doing that, then no wonder you would not want to continue. Perhaps you tend to see one person as making all the demands and the other as the victim of that. Of course you are right and I do demand money and words from you, but maybe we can look at the demands that you

107

might want to make on me.' The patient looked surprised and said, 'Well you're right; if I was going to stay I would want some things changed. It wouldn't just be me that would have to change.' There is still not much hint of co-operation or mutuality here, but there is a beginning of some sort of thought process about what goes on between two people.

The therapist is valuing relationship and thinking with more than a simplistic view of autonomy. If the goal were merely that the patient could make a decision to leave, she could have greeted the patient's announcement with encouragement and wished her well. On the other hand, to take autonomy at such a level would be to ignore its rational component. Erwin (1997: 30) defines autonomy as:

- the capacity for rational reflection
- the tendency to eliminate defective desires
- the capacity for self-control.

It is of course possible to hold a simplistic view of autonomy which says that being able to leave the therapist might be the patient's major act of freedom. Erwin's definition allows for the need of the patient to be able to decide when to leave, but adds to that the idea that the patient who has achieved sufficient autonomy will be right in wishing to do so, because the effect of therapy will have been to remove defective desires. This may well be the case with successful therapy, but how do we know whether the therapy has been successful? The difficulty is that the patient is unlikely to know that his desires are defective and the therapist will have to decide whether he or she knows better. In practice, this is done through counter-transference responses in the therapist which indicate how much anxiety and hostility remain, as well as from accounts of changes in the external life situation. In Bion's terms, the therapist will have enabled the patient to reach a point where the processes of introjection and projection have successfully diminished the infantile terrors and rages to the point where the patient can allow ideas to come together and create new thoughts (Bion 1967).

Valuing the therapist's views

When the patient expresses a desire to leave which the therapist finds premature, in that this stage of integration has not yet been

108

reached in his view, we return to the question of whether or not the therapist might claim a privileged status in that he has some knowledge that the patient does not have. Psychoanalysis in the early days would probably have had no problem in claiming this status for the analyst. Subsequently, writers such as Carl Rogers (1951) have emphasised the patient's conscious knowledge and have taken the view that the patient does have both the knowledge and the authority to make the most useful choices. Nevertheless, the therapist needs to maintain the view that he has some expertise, even if he embraces the view that we are working with two subjectivities in the room. There is still a need to claim some skill or knowledge for the therapist, or why, as Gabbard (1997) points out, are patients bothering to pay us and attend sessions? He also argues that patients want the therapist to know more, and to see what the patient himself misses.

The therapist cannot become the desired wise parent and may indeed wish to enable the patient to move to a more self-activating state, but it would be difficult to argue that the therapist is wrong to use such skill and knowledge as he does have. Using experience might entail saying something different about ending and not accepting the view of the patient. This can still stop short of the objective view, that the therapist is always, by virtue of skill and training, more objective, and therefore right. Hanly (1995) believes that we must integrate objectivity and subjectivity so that the therapist may have perhaps more objectivity in his subjectivity. On the other hand, an element of subjectivity reminds us of the fluidity of the analytic situation. The possibility of any kind of certainty eludes us. Because we are always likely to be caught by our own subjectivity we must retain a view that the therapist, because of his or her own training, therapy, supervision, experience, etc., is still in a privileged position and therefore sometimes more able to see what is needed than the patient, but equally must always be tentative and willing to be convinced otherwise.

Hinshelwood (1997) deals with a specific case in which he had a patient who decided to marry soon after she entered analysis. She had a satisfactory intellectual relationship but was not attracted to the man sexually. The question for the analyst was whether to advise her, as Freud might have done, to suspend her life for the time being, and not to embark on marriage while in the turmoil of the early stages of analysis. He decided that he would not do that but was

also grappling with the question of whether she was effec-
tively ending the analysis: telling him that she had found
her own cure, by avoiding the issue of sexuality altogether.
In fact she chose to continue to come to the sessions, and
a way was discovered to enhance her ability to live her life
while remaining in analysis.

(Hinshelwood 1997: 90–91)

The choice presented is not only whether therapy enhances life
or precludes it, although that is an important issue for those who
do long-term work in particular. The therapist will have to judge
the extent to which the patient is capable of making a rational choice
with a large degree of consciousness that takes into account external
reality and is not driven by pathological defences. Because therapy
may disturb the existing defences, it may bring a period of chaos
in which making major life decisions is not a good idea. On the
other hand, patients who get better will show this by being able to
move forward. Fortunately, the decision does not always depend on
the therapist's judgement, although a comment may turn out to be
very powerful.

Valuing mutuality

If autonomy is not just a matter of making decisions for oneself,
but does also include being able to make decisions from a position
of as much self-awareness as possible, it must also include being
able to see the other as a separate individual with views that may
or may not be valid. This implies a change in the patient's valuing
processes such that the ending can be a matter of negotiation and
discussion. The very fact that a patient does not make absolute,
unilateral decisions is itself a criterion for readiness to leave. In the
case of Mrs S, there is only a hint of that faculty developing. The
therapist would be led both by counter-transference feeling response
and by a process of rational thought to conclude that she has not
yet reached a level of functioning that can be considered to be truly
autonomous.

Mutuality cannot be left to the patient's developmental process
alone. It is an area in which the therapist must also change to a
position in which, without abdicating from the necessary degree of
responsibility for the therapy and what happens in it, he begins to
see a greater possibility of accepting the patient's ability to judge
his own functioning. This involves not only being able to overcome

his own disinclination to allow the therapy to end but also being willing to accept that the patient may be right in wishing to leave, even when the therapist is not sure or believes the contrary. This can happen only when the overall functioning of the patient has reached a point of stability and self-awareness that the particular therapist can recognise as healthy. It therefore depends on the therapist being able to change the boundaries of his own faith and confidence with each new ending.

Valuing difference

Whatever the therapist's values, he is likely to seek convergence from the patient in order to judge her ready to leave. The therapist must also be prepared to learn how to work with the patient who is clearly different from herself. Not surprisingly, overt differences in the perceived physical body, such as skin colour or disability, or the more diffuse areas of culture or sexuality, may be a genuine difficulty for either or both people. Alternatively, overt differences may be used as the vehicle for conveying other hidden difficulties. There is no doubt that most therapists will have difficulty with some aspect of difference. Conscious values might not always be reflected in actions. In working with a patient when there is a noticeable difference in, for example, age, the difference must be recognised overtly and be part of the therapeutic dialogue. In that way it is less likely to form a potential reason for a sudden ending.

Therapists might prefer that the problems were all in the patient, but few would deny that there will be areas of difference where they find it particularly hard to face for themselves what the meaning of the difference might be. There will be some inevitable difficulties in understanding each other which may be enough to bring about a premature ending if they are not addressed. There may be times when a therapist is simply not able to understand enough and the patient needs a referral to another therapist where the differences will not provide such an initial obstacle. An even more difficult crisis will arise when the perceived difference is in the therapist. For example, if the therapist is visibly disabled or blind, the patient may find it very difficult to say how he or she feels about it and may simply not come back. Yet this is an ending that could sometimes be avoided, and therapists who know that they are seen as different are likely to confront it immediately. Therapists with less obvious characteristics will have a more difficult time because they will not know how much they are affecting any given patient.

111

Lack of shame in the therapist is one of the most important qualities in this context, where early acknowledgement is usually the only way to avoid a precipitous ending.

Patients may be extremely anxious about the therapist's values in any given area. There may be particular difficulties over sexuality, which the assessment should bring to the surface. In an analytic setting, the patient may have questions which remain unanswered and he will have to put up with assumptions about the therapist's sexuality which may not be confirmed or denied. Both patient and therapist will try to discover each other's values, although the therapist has the advantage in the assessment session of discovering more overtly what the patient thinks and feels. Patients try to deduce what they can of the therapist's values from any available hints.

Attitudes to the value of life and death are also of central importance where conflicts need to be made overt. In reinforcing the choice for life or in accepting death for another, the therapist may have absolute values that life is always the right choice or may have criteria for the quality of life. The therapist's views of what is right may have to change during the course of a therapy or may be so rigid that the patient leaves in despair. Patients will often deduce conclusions about the therapist's values which may or may not be right, but may come up against genuine differences which prevent suicide and death from being explored as the patient needs them to be. The therapist's attitude towards suicide is further discussed in Chapter 7.

The patient who threatens suicide out of anger provides that therapist with a potentially difficult ending and tries to force the therapist to choose between struggling on with work that might have become counter-productive and an ending that might be full of anger and hostility. Ethical difficulties arise when the borderline or narcissistic patient creates an intensely negative transference and, like the child in a dysfunctional family, cannot leave. The therapist may have been enduring intense hate or erotic demands for some time and may strongly wish for an ending.

> Ms U was a patient who formed a passionate erotic attachment to her therapist. The hatred that the protestations of love were intended to conceal was never acknowledged, and the gifts, hanging about outside the consulting room, etc. that constituted constant attempts to act out over many months did not diminish, even though the therapist

was patient and empathic while making a steady effort to interpret the controlling omnipotence that seemed to be developing. When the therapist finally said, 'I do not think that you are able or willing to work with me and therefore I think we must fix a time to finish,' the patient immediately threatened to kill herself. The therapist had to exercise considerable courage to try to say that in spite of this threat, there would still have to be an ending. In this case the therapist's courage was rewarded, and the ending phase, although tempestuous and frequently frightening for both, did lead to some fruitful work and a parting between two living people. In this case, one of the functions of the threat of suicide had been to deprive the unsatisfying therapist of a satisfying ending.

There is a second group of patients who themselves threaten to end both therapy and their own lives without the therapist having mentioned ending. These are likely to be patients who are depressed and who are therefore seeking oblivion, fusion with a mother at such a primitive level that she would have no chance ever to reject. There are difficult technical questions here about how to do the work, but there are also questions about how the therapist values the patient's view of the desirability of death and ending. Sometimes a patient wishes to die, and no matter how much a therapist may wish it were otherwise, nothing can prevent the death.

There is a third group of suicidal patients who choose suicide as an ending to unbearable suffering. Therapists who work with the terminally ill are often needed to work with a patient over the question of whether death can be left to come naturally or whether it will be chosen. No therapist is likely to wish to set rules for every case, and sometimes we will be profoundly moved by a patient's need to reach an end.

In all these cases, the therapist has to work with the need to value the patient's right to choose death, but will also have to struggle with profound feelings about the question.

Mr V, a man aged 75, came to therapy, having been referred by his GP for depression. He had taken every kind of anti-depressant in the pharmacy but was apparently untouched by them. He was a sensitive, intelligent man, a writer who was no longer able to write. He said that his one longing was to die. He thought about ways to kill

himself every day and said that he had the correct combi-
nation of drugs for certain death when he chose it. In the
meantime I was to be given a chance, once a week, to
convince him that life was worth living. His history involved
a powerful, controlling mother who had not valued his
father at all. Mr V had become a bomber pilot in the Second
World War and had conducted many successful bombing
raids on Germany. During one of these his fiancée had
been killed in a German bombing raid on London. He said
he had convinced himself that he had killed her, although
this was not a psychotic delusion and rationally he knew
that he had not.

The first part of the therapy was spent in an attempt to
analyse away this guilt. This was completely fruitless and
at the end of every session he would say, 'See you next
week – if I'm still alive.' I felt great pressure to come up
with whatever it was that he wanted from me, but of course
neither of us knew what that was. I did begin to understand that the first requirement was that I should stay alive
and not let him kill me off in despair. There were times
when I was very angry with him and felt like saying that
he should just get on and kill himself, but mostly I felt a
great desire for him to stay alive. This I interpreted as his
own split desire for life versus the longing for death as a
respite from the whole struggle. When I acknowledged that
I experienced these two sets of feelings, something
changed, and he was able to talk to me about death in a
way he had not before. He told me that he knew it was
his way of trying to get me to see that he had some power.
In other words, his mother had seen him as weak and I
must see him as powerful, even if only in the ability to
make me feel that he might kill himself.

There was another part of him that needed attention.
He had been a bomber pilot, and one of his most powerful
memories was of flying a small fighter plane under a
bridge just after he had learned of the death of his fiancée.
He knew this had been a very dangerous act, both for
himself and others, and he thought that he had wished
to kill himself then but had not put it into words. We
established that the pilot in him was his rational self,
extremely perceptive and skilled but at times hijacked by
his powerful anger and destructiveness. Gradually his

depression changed to anger. My fear that he could never end therapy without killing himself diminished, and after three years he did decide to stop. He was still inclined to depression but was no longer threatening suicide. He said that therapy had not done much for him but at least he was able to see that the pilot in him could be of some value and use. I received a card from a friend of his some years later to say that he had died of a stroke after writing his autobiography.

This case illustrates both the difficulty for the therapist of working with a very suicidal patient and the importance of achieving a kind of autonomy in which there is some reduction of omnipotence. The pilot in Mr V was unstoppable to begin with and was totally isolated in his cockpit. It was only after the acknowledgement of some dependence that a more useful autonomy was achieved in which he could manage to fly on his own.

Conclusion

In practice, therefore, therapists find that there is not one truth for all, but many different aspects of truth. Autonomy is a criterion for ending insofar as it shows the patient arriving at a kind of truth for himself. Where the patient is sufficiently independent to consider ending, but wishes to take the therapist's view into account, that will in itself indicate that the patient may be functioning at a more mature level. In some cases, the patient will end in an omnipotent, unilateral way, either through leaving or sometimes through death. In any case, the therapist's job will be to seek the truth of what is happening, as far as that is possible. If the truth is that the therapist is following selfish needs of her own, that must be faced and dealt with. Mrs S (p. 107) suspects that her therapist is valuing her own economic welfare above that of Mrs S. Sometimes such factors are bound to enter into the therapist's attitude. Even if personal desires for money or status were to be eliminated, the therapist's task in assessing readiness to end is not an easy one, and each therapist will have to work out what is true to the best of her ability. In Chapter 7 I will examine the way in which ethical codes relate to values and govern the ending process.

References

Balint, M. (1968) *The Basic Fault*, London: Tavistock.

Bentham, J. (1789) *The Principles of Morals and Legislation*, (Reprinted 1988) New York: Phoenix Books.

Bion, W. R. (1967) *Second Thoughts*, London: Karnac (Reprinted 1984.)

Erwin, E. (1997) *Philosophy and Psychotherapy*, London: Sage.

Freud, S. (1920) 'Beyond the pleasure principle', *SE* 18.

Gabbard, G. (1997) 'A reconsideration of objectivity in the analyst', *International Journal of Psycho-analysis* 78: 15.

Hanly, C. (1995) 'On facts and ideas in psycho-analysis', *International Journal of Psycho-analysis* 76: 5.

Hinshelwood, R. D. (1997) *Therapy or Coercion*, London: Karnac.

Holmes, J. and Lindley, R. (1989) *The Values of Psychotherapy*, Oxford: Oxford University Press.

Mill, J. S. (1861) Reprinted in *Utilitarianism*, London: Fontana.

Rogers, C. (1951) *Client Centred Therapy*, London: Constable. (Reprinted 1987.)

7

ENDS AND MEANS
The ethics of ending

Psychotherapy has a body of knowledge about human nature and sets of techniques that are derived from theory or sometimes are simply pragmatic. Some work and others do not. Sometimes the achievements of psychotherapy are brought about by the charismatic force of the therapist's personality and faith and sometimes by a very routine application of well-known and tested methods. The necessary existence of the former element, the power of the individual therapist, in both the relationship and the process, is such that ethical thinking and the restraints of ethical codes are always necessary, although not always sufficient. As soon as ethical principles conflict, codes become useless and we are thrown back on individual morality.

Ethics is in the public arena where morality becomes the law that must be followed. Therapists must adhere to these rules but must learn how to apply them to the individual who will make unique demands. Psychotherapy is about setting boundaries and changing the ones that are inappropriate. These are not only the boundaries between individuals in a given society and culture, but also the boundaries within the individual that prevent the free movement of thought and feeling within the psyche. The therapist may be allowed a privileged position, in that the normal social fences have to be taken down so that a stranger may be told the most intimate details of a patient's life, love and sexuality. This freedom of movement implies a particular need for restraint. The lack of normal boundaries paradoxically implies a particular need for specific and strong boundaries in the therapist. It is often the failure to establish boundaries that are appropriate to the therapeutic process and to a particular individual that leads to untimely and contested endings in therapy.

Therapists using models that seek to analyse a transference relationship have particularly difficult ethical questions to answer, usually about boundaries, and they will very often find only minimal guidance in ethical codes, since these can legislate only for behaviour that is clearly and grossly harmful. Where there is a question of competence or dubious technique, the codes are often of no help. In this chapter I will also look at the therapist's use of self and the degree of opacity or openness that is used in the ending phase. Other areas of technique with ethical implications, especially for ending, are connected with the degree of confidentiality both during the ending and after it. In different ways, these are implied by theoretical models and are certainly used in different ways by individual therapists.

The ending process is subject to strife between patient and therapist. The number of complaints and appeals received by the United Kingdom Council for Psychotherapy (UKCP) and the British Association for Counselling that are connected with an ending that went wrong provides adequate testimony to the importance of considering the ethics of the therapist's behaviour in this area. At the time of writing all the members of the United Kingdom Council for Psychotherapy are organisations, each of which must construct its own codes of ethics and practice to suit its own model of psychotherapy. These codes must be written to comply with the basic requirements set out by UKCP. The reason for not having one single centralised code has been the need for different working practices required, for example, by those working with children and those working with couples or groups. In these modalities the need for different codes of practice is obvious. Children may not be able to make a necessary complaint for themselves, and third-party complaints will be both reasonable and necessary. In work with adults the question of whether, for example, partners are entitled to complain about treatment which has caused them problems is much more debatable. They would often wish for the therapy to end. Such complaints cannot usually be heard without breaking the confidentiality of the patient, and most organisations refuse to hear them on those grounds. Such complaints are likely to relate to endings outside of therapy such as the breakup of families or partnerships where the therapist is thought to have great influence and has not stopped the work. In cases where relationships outside are ending, the therapist has responsibility to work at the patient's understanding of the issue, and not to try to impose his own agenda.

Different models of psychotherapy may also need different codes of practice. In some models the contract has a time-limit and the ethical issue is to keep to the contract. This in itself is not always easy, as there may be the temptation to prolong the work into private practice (see Chapter 9). Each model has its logic. A humanistic therapist will be placing great reliance on the autonomy of the patient in making the decision to end (see Chapter 6). An analytical therapist hopes to convert the resolution or solution of the imaginary relationship into something more mutual. Particular codes will be required for those who use massage or other forms of touch. Behavioural therapy and paradoxical therapy need to make clear what informed consent might mean for them and what must be said in making a contract.

Analytical therapists who have been working by means of interpreting current events as transferred from the past to connect them overtly or implicitly with the patient's mother, father, siblings and significant others, not to mention parts of the self, will become intimately involved in the patient's life and emotions. The delicate balance that allows the patient to feel disappointed, frustrated, angry and yet stay in therapy may not be maintained, and the patient may tip over into psychosis or leave and make a complaint. Complaints often focus on the therapist's sudden or apparently sudden decision to end the therapy when the patient is in the midst of powerful feelings. There will be questions about whether adequate provision was made for other referrals or at least contact with the general practitioner or psychiatric service. Investigators may be faced with the question: Was the therapist behaving competently and ethically or not? If not, there will be the possibility of sanctions, the most extreme of course being the loss of registration and the ability to practise under the auspices of the professional body. As we do not have statutory regulation of the profession at the time of writing, anyone may continue to practise as a therapist no matter what complaints have been made and substantiated, but to do so would be difficult.

The ethics of technique

Klimovsky, Dupetit and Zysman (1995) have written on the question of whether there is a logical connection between the ends of psychological treatment, its techniques and its ethics. We must have good reasons for the rules that we impose on ourselves and our patients. Klimovsky *et al.* look at the chain of reasoning that lies beneath an ethical statement. Statements of fact and ethical statements can be mixed in a way that is confusing. For example, 'The unjust is ethically bad' is a purely ethical statement, whereas 'An unjust action committed by a man towards another results in a particular kind of conduct or symptom' is a mixed factual and ethical statement (Klimovsky *et al.* 1995: 981). If we mix these sorts of statements unintentionally we are unlikely to be able to arrive at clear conclusions about what is the case and what we should do.

These authors point to the difference between the two uses of the word *must*. It can be used to imply that a certain course of action is necessary in order to achieve a certain end or goal. Alternatively, it can be used to convey an ethical imperative. They look in particular at the importance of ethics in interpreting what is considered in analytical work as patterns of behaviour transferred from the past. They construct the following chain of reasoning:

- The transference is the expression of an unconscious tendency to repeat forms of behaviour from infancy brought into the present in the relationship with the analyst (theoretical statement).
- Transference manifestations are observed in every psycho-analytic treatment (a factual statement).
- The analyst *must* analyse the patient's transference manifestations in order to understand his past (a mixed ethical statement).
- It is good for the analyst to *analyse* his patient's transference (an ethical statement).

(Klimovsky *et al.* 1995: 981)

Freud's view was that understanding the hidden roots of a neurosis was an intrinsic good, as in the last statement, and although he abandoned the technique of hypnosis as a tool to discover what the patient had hidden in his psyche, he nevertheless advocated a powerfully silent therapist sitting out of sight and waiting for the patient to reveal himself. This technique is based on a logical sequence which says that it is curative to come upon the memories or desires that are hidden and to admit them to consciousness. The technique of a silent analyst encouraging free association allows unconscious memories and wishes to surface or to make themselves known in the gaps, the patterns of repetition, the *faux pas*, etc.; with this basic premise, the logic of ethics would lead to the conclusion that the technique is good. Nevertheless, many patients who make complaints cite a therapist who was not sufficiently 'warm' or 'human'. The argument of the end justifying the means does not seem to be valid in this case, because if the patient cannot endure the deprivation of the method, the end will not be achieved anyway.

A depriving analytic attitude contrasts with the current view of many analytical practitioners that the process of therapy involves the meeting of two subjects and their effect on each other. Jung's alchemical metaphor has long since emphasised the need to be open to the melting down that occurs when two people meet over a fairly long period. Increasing interest in intersubjectivity has now entered into mainstream psychoanalysis. Roger Kennedy in his book on the nature of subjectivity (1998) emphasises that the therapist may be natural or spontaneous, that being neutral is not being neutered. He points out that the therapist may succumb to the fear of seduction. The therapist suffers not only from the fear of sexual seduction but also from the anxiety of being deceived, duped, 'taken for a ride' by the patient (1998: 113). This is the sort of fear that can lead to the practice of defensive psychotherapy in which the therapist's main concern is not to get into trouble (Clarkson and Murdin 1996).

Clarkson has also written on the temptation of the psychotherapist to stand aside from anything that is difficult in the social, cultural or political context. She points out that the whole profession suffers from an unhealthy narcissism if it is absorbed by its own image to the extent that therapists ignore both what is going on outside the consulting room and also at times some of what is going on inside it. She adds that in some political situations, such as recently in South Africa or earlier in Germany, one might understand that active involvement would require extreme personal bravery. Usually we are called upon only to be willing to enter into the struggles that are going on in the room. Being in the room can be dangerous enough however, so it is not surprising that therapists are sometimes too zealous in obeying the rules. Too much preoccupation with the technical rules may at times be as dangerous as ignoring them. Clarkson and Murdin (1996) wrote about the importance of the spirit of the law rather than the letter. When it comes to subjectivity and to deciding what is permissible in the therapeutic situation, we may have to observe the spirit of the law rather than the letter.

An ethical question arises if a patient is finding the silence of an analytic approach difficult. A technically correct approach might mean that no hint can be given that the analyst cares how the patient feels or whether the patient gets better. Of course, too much emphasis on getting better can lead to a risk of the patient trying to please the therapist or alternatively trying to frustrate him. On the other hand, the therapist may sometimes be the only one who can maintain some hope, and at times this may need to be conveyed to the patient. In the ending phase this may require particular attention because after a long therapy, most people will go through various different degrees of doubt, hope, optimism and despair. Some therapists consider that they should become more open and deliberately remove the veil of mystery that has surrounded them. This would imply a deliberate and planned attempt to dissolve parental transference and become more ordinary.

Passionate attachment and the destructive ending

The process of therapy may be regarded as the process of finding and dissolving transferred feelings that are not appropriate in the present. If this is not done continuously or if the patient has developed the kind of embedded erotic feelings described in Chapter 5, the therapist would have to find a way of ending that is ethical. A transference of this sort is as likely to be strengthened as dissolved by revelations by the therapist about his or her personal life or beliefs. An equally dangerous alternative is for the therapist to withdraw. Sometimes the patient offers gifts and allurements which the unwary may accept. When the whole thing gets out of hand and the supervisor says it should stop, the patient may well feel totally rejected and unable to cope. In this situation the therapist may bring about the ending of the therapy either overtly or indirectly through fear. Patients often make complaints about these endings. In such a case, it is the initial encouragement of the transference that went too far and became at least unwise if not unethical. Assessment of the potential for such lethal passionate attachments is not infallible, but must be attempted in order to protect patients and inexperienced therapists.

Psychotherapy organisations have great difficulty in dealing with the aftermath of such endings. Patients are profoundly hurt and wish only to prolong the relationship with the therapist. They do this through a long-drawn-out complaints and appeals process. The therapist fears litigation or the risk of losing professional credibility or even registration, and refuses to have any further contact with the patient. This absolute prohibition infuriates and frustrates the patient even more. No one is very good at dealing with these situations. Perhaps the only answer is to provide some sort of mediation or couple therapy for a therapeutic relationship that is in this sort of difficulty before it ends disastrously. At least there might be some way of helping the patient to find another therapist with whom the connection might be less dangerously passionate.

Therapists know they need to be consistent, and yet that knowledge has to be balanced against the need to learn from the patient and change when appropriate. The change has to be carefully planned and thought through. The necessary change that comes from learning during the process is very different from the sudden change imposed in an attempt to improve or facilitate the ending process. The case of Mr W illustrates the difficulty of sudden change at the end:

A therapist, Mr W, was seeing a woman aged 34, Ms X. She had been coming to him for four years and had done some very useful work on her difficulties in relating to men. Her presenting problem had been sexual abuse by a step-father when she was about 8 years old. Ms X had been overtly erotic in her behaviour in the therapy and Mr W had felt the need for very rigorous boundaries which he had held successfully. As a result, Ms X had ceased to try to seduce him or to complain about his hardness of heart. Mr W thought that she was much better and when she spoke about the possibility that she might marry a man she knew at work who wished to leave the area for a promotion in the next year or so, he suggested that they should end the therapy.

Ms X agreed that they should end in about six months' time and before she got married. After a few sessions, she began to show signs of regretting the decision and became more and more depressed. She was failing to meet dead-lines at work and was turning up late for sessions. Mr W said that he supposed Ms X might be frightened about how she would manage without the sessions. She agreed and said that she would not be able to manage without Mr W. She had changed her mind about her engagement and did not think she could marry her fiancé after all.

Mr W then grew worried that Ms X had more powerful feelings for him than he had recognised. In something of a panic, he decided to stick to the ending date that had been arranged and in the sessions decided to make her more aware of his failings and weaknesses so that she would not idealise him so much. He began to say things like 'I understand that you feel attached to me but of course you do not know what I am really like.' She mentioned on one occasion that she liked the way he could speak so deci-sively. He then said, 'Oh well, I do not always make good decisions. The other week I decided to paint the outside of the house, as you can see [many comments had been made about the painting by most of the patients], but I am already regretting the colour and I don't think I chose the best people to do it as they haven't finished yet.' Ms X seemed somewhat shocked by this departure from his usual restraint but said nothing for the rest of the session.

At the next session Ms X handed Mr W a piece of paper on which she had written the name of a firm of decorators run by her brother. Mr W said that he was grateful for the suggestion but did not think it appropriate that he should change decorators. Clearly this was an avoidance. What was inappropriate was that he should discuss decorating in a connubial way with a patient. His intention to make the ending easier was simply digging him a deeper hole from which to escape. He had to acknowledge that talking to Ms X about the decorating was speaking in a way that he had not done before, and that she might have experienced it as his encouragement to change the nature of their relationship. She agreed that she had. He then said that he intended to maintain his position as her therapist and any improvements in the future would have to be those that she carried out on herself.

In this case, ending therapy is very difficult for the patient who has fallen in love with the imaginary therapist. Inexperienced therapists may well encourage this kind of adoration and may themselves be excited by it. On the other hand, an inexperienced therapist may not notice that it is happening until he or she is in the thick of it. As Mr W pointed out, the patient does not know the therapist as a whole person and is in love with an ideal, tolerant, non-retaliating father or mother. Clearly this imaginary relationship should have been analysed throughout the work, if that were possible. The feeling and its intensity is totally absorbing to the patient and is likely to send the therapist into a panic when he or she realises the degree of intensity of feeling.

Ethical codes cannot specify technique: they usually say only what we should not do. There are no universal rules about how to deal with the patient who falls in love or in hate. Each model of psychotherapy will have its own solutions or recommendations. The bottom-line statement is usually that the therapist must not exploit the patient. Exploitation implies using power inappropriately. Even attempts to dissolve the kind of relationship that has developed may turn into an inappropriate use of power. The most important way for the therapist to decline to take on too much power is to be honest with the patient. This does not imply too much self-revelation but does imply a complete lack of pretence. Whatever is said must be genuine. The ideal must be that the therapist helps the patient to stay in a fluid state in which love and hate are available but there is still some understanding that the therapist is not the beloved mother or father or potential partner, while allowing the kind of exploration that Freud referred to when he said that the patient shows what he or she is like in love and the doctor shows the patient this image (Freud 1914). The only hope is in the skill and humanity of the therapist who can keep the balance and enable the patient to do the same. A total refusal to take on the role of the beloved is essential and, as for Mr W above, this sometimes means falling into traps, but always trying to put into words what is happening and what has happened. The ending cannot be forced or made into an ideal resolution. It will often remain messy and unsatisfactory, and no amount of making oneself ordinary at the last minute will help if the therapist has not been ordinary all along.

Confidentiality

One of the main values in psychotherapy is the confidentiality of the therapeutic relationship. The great majority of patients would not be able or willing to unburden themselves of the kinds of problems they bring to a therapist if they did not believe that the problems would remain within the relative safety of the minds of the two people concerned. Many therapists also seek supervision or consultation, and will let patients know that this aspect of the work is also confidential but does extend the boundary of who knows about the work. For most patients supervision is welcome and reduces the fear of abuse. Where there is only one parent there can be a secret and abusive relationship, but the second parent may be able to control and make the other safe. The supervisor is often seen to adopt the role of the other parent (see Chapter 9).

In the ending process, supervision or consultation often becomes a necessity if there is doubt about the appropriateness of the ending. As long as this is provided in the contract, it is perfectly ethical. There may however be other aspects of the ending process where confidentiality is threatened by the therapist. In the United States, confidentiality is under constant threat because of legislation that requires therapists to report sexual abuse as well as any possible involvement with criminal activity or any predictable crime. There are therefore many situations in which a therapist may have to stop a patient and point out that the information that he or she is giving may make it necessary for the therapist to speak to a statutory authority. Bollas and Sundelson (1995) have written about the problem this poses for the future of this profession which depends on the possibility of privacy.

In the UK at present, there is less pressure to report except in the case of ongoing abuse of children or of a potential act of terrorism. We are not likely to encounter the case where a thera-pist says, 'If you tell me about that, I shall have to report what you say to the police, social workers, etc.' Yet there are certainly cases where a therapist may need to deliver some sort of ultimatum. For example, if a patient were to tell the therapist that she felt in danger of hitting her children, the therapist might be torn between two ethical imperatives. On the one hand, the children might need protection. The mother might not want anyone to know of her predicament because she is afraid that the children will be taken away from her. Yet the therapist now knows. He or she must decide whether the children's potential danger weighs more heavily than the needs of the patient and the potential to help her if the therapy is preserved. If the therapist insists on breaking the confi-dentiality, the therapy may come to a premature end. The ideal solution is that the therapist can work with the patient while helping her to seek the support of an agency because practical help may well be needed. On the other hand, it is also true that any admis-sion of the sorts of violent feelings that might be problematic will also be quite likely to lead to children being put on the 'at risk' register and possibly removed or given to the care of a partner. The Code of Ethics of the British Association for Counselling is very clear and explicit about the priorities in making these boundaries. Although there may be a legal duty to report ongoing sexual abuse of minors, the patient's confidentiality must never be broken and an ending risked without extremely good reason.

Publication of material about patients is another area of ethical dif-ficulty. Most therapists would probably prefer to write about ongo-ing or recent work in which the atmosphere, the detail, is fresh in the mind. On the other hand, the mere fact of asking the patient's per-mission and having the therapist's thoughts and the patient's mater-ial set out in print for all to see will have an effect on the ongoing work, which is undesirable because it is introduced purely to satisfy a desire of the therapist. The alternative is to wait until the work is ended and then ask for permission to publish. This leads into a grey area when the patient cannot be found and therefore permission cannot be obtained. In most cases disguise is sufficient, especially where publications are likely to be read only within the profession. Nevertheless, therapists must adopt the principle that a patient is always a patient in the sense of being entitled to privacy. Even when the work is ended, the therapist does not own the experience.

The threat of suicide is another situation in which questions of confidentiality must be faced. I have discussed the conflict of values that it raises in Chapter 6. Robert Firestone (1997) has written of the indications and possible treatment of suicidal patients. He points out that the therapist is likely to experience strong feelings when with a suicidal patient. This will come as no surprise to most of us:

> suicidal patients often provoke feelings of dislike, discom-
> fort, even malice in therapists. Negative feelings that
> suicidal patients feel towards themselves are evoked in the
> therapist during sessions or interviews.
>
> (1997: 237)

Firestone considers that such feelings in the therapist should alert one to the possibility of suicide if there has been any suicidal ideation already or if there are other factors leading to a suspicion of suicidal intention. We may all arrive at the conclusion that a particular patient is at risk. A much more difficult problem arises if the patient is not willing to talk about a suicidal intention or is willing to talk to the therapist but to no one else.

Firestone does not take this to be a particularly serious problem, as he is writing in the context of an open and family-orientated approach to psychotherapy. He says:

> Clinicians should warn the patient's family and significant
> others of the patient's suicidal potential and enlist their
> involvement in management and treatment unless such
> involvement is contra-indicated by toxic family interac-
> tions. Providing information during the course of treatment
> can lead to active collaboration and help in monitoring
> the patient's and family's distress. In terms of the legal
> aspects of suicide the family is less likely to bring suit
> against clinicians who have previously established good
> relations with them.
>
> (1997: 241)

Firestone also points out the importance of keeping notes of the work:

> Defensive clinical notes written after the fact may help somewhat in damage control but there is no substitute for a timely thoughtful and complete record that demonstrates . . . a knowledge of the epidemiology, risk factors and treatment literature for the suicidal patient.
>
> (1997: 240)

Not all therapists would agree with the importance of keeping detailed notes of the sort recommended here, but although the choice will reflect the personality of the therapist and will therefore have a part to play in the therapy, it is not likely to affect the course or speed of the ending itself. In the event of actual suicide or a sudden conflicted ending, it is certainly possible that the therapist will be required to produce a record of the treatment and might be accused of negligence if no such record is available.

Therapists working with patients who refuse to speak to their families and do not wish the therapist to do so will be in the difficult position of having to hold confidentiality as a value to be preserved if at all possible. Against this will stand the possibility that an insistence on informing others of the danger without the patient's consent or in direct contravention of his wishes may lead to the end of the therapy. Hidden within this dilemma may lie the therapist's response to the patient's hate and anger and his wish for the patient to die. Being told that you are not good enough to prevent someone from wishing to take his or her life is bound to arouse in the therapist feelings of anger and a wish to retaliate. Retaliation can take many forms, but one might well be the betrayal of the patient through unnecessary breaches of confidentiality. Another aspect of the same response could be the desperate need to enlist others in the blame, hate and anger that surrounds, if only at an unconscious level, the threats of suicide. Rejection is bound to be in the therapist's feelings somewhere because suicidal potential is always a rejection of the living. This rejection needs to be explored in the therapist, and in the patient's own experience, rather than acted out by the therapist.

Firestone (1997) cites as an error committed by a therapist the delivery of an ultimatum along the lines: 'If you make an attempt at suicide, I shall discontinue the treatment.' This is a clear acting out of the rejection that the patient has no doubt experienced at some time in the past and wishes to impose on the therapist who rejects it and hands it back. There may be times when it is possible and necessary to hand it back in the sense of talking to the patient about this rejection and what it implies. After the patient has been given a chance to make use of opportunities to work on these memories in the therapy, he or she may still persist in suicide attempts and the therapist may eventually decide that the anxiety is unbearable and the hostility cannot be reduced in that therapy. Therapists have their limits and may not be able or willing to continue, although ending in such circumstances should always be a last resort.

Referral to someone more experienced or to an agency such as a hospital may be all that is possible. Firestone cites a case in which a referral to another therapist was made, but before contact was arranged with the new therapist, the patient shot himself after being sent home from hospital (1997: 244). Referral to another therapist may work, but it is not an easy or obvious solution. The loss of the previous therapist may be too much to bear. Referral to hospital may be easier because the therapist may be able to continue to see the patient at least when he or she is discharged, and because there will be a much safer holding environment while it lasts. Referral is a process which inevitably raises the problem of the patient's consent to it and to information being passed to the next therapist. Is it ethical to refer a highly suicidal patient to a colleague without telling the colleague about the problem? If the patient does not agree to the release of information, the therapist will again have to decide between conflicting ethical imperatives because the possible outcome of a new therapy may depend on a certain amount of information being passed on. GPs and psychiatrists will often not require or use information from psychotherapists even if it is available. Unfortunately, hospital stays are harder to obtain and often shorter in duration than we might wish, and there may not be time to discover what the problems are, even if there are staff qualified to do so.

When there is a risk of ending through suicide, supervision or consultation is essential and it is difficult to see how one could argue against it in these cases, but discussions that go outside that area without the patient's permission might sometimes be an avoidance of confronting negative emotions in the patient. For example, the therapist may well feel in need of extra support and may find it tempting to talk to colleagues more freely than is appropriate or may talk to the patient's family without obtaining consent in an attempt to gain support and get rid of the feelings of isolation and rejection which must in fact, as far as possible, remain within the therapy as part of the work.

Firestone (1997) looks at the possibility of forming an anti-suicide contract with a patient. He sees such a contract as potentially useful in assessing the patient's motivation and willingness to accept a degree of responsibility for the treatment. It is a comfort to the therapist in all sorts of ways: it implies safety for the therapy as well as a formal alliance with the patient. It may provide for the ending of the therapy if the contract is broken and this will salve the therapist's conscience if the work becomes unbearable. There is nothing unethical about such a contract if the patient understands it clearly, but there is a question about the morality of abandoning the person whose problem is so severe that he or she cannot keep to a contract that was presumably made in good faith. A second problem with such contracts is that, as Firestone points out, it may lull the therapist into a false sense of security. Indications of change in mood or intention should be carefully monitored at all times.

In this section I have looked at some of the difficulties raised by the suicidal patient in the constant threat of ending that they pose to the therapist. They can induce the therapist to make a premature ending either deliberately or through actions that lead the patient to walk out. These difficulties are of course intensified with the suicidal patient but are not unique to these cases. All therapeutic work is subject to the dangers of the therapist who acts out of counter-transference emotions rather than bringing them back to the work and making them available to thought and to language.

The patient deserves an ending

The ethical practice of psychotherapy implies the kind of endings that must be avoided and also implies that therapists have an ethical obligation to keep ending in mind and be prepared to help patients to end appropriately. The British Association for Counselling Code of Ethics for Counsellors, as revised in September 1997, states that:

> Counsellors work with clients to reach a recognised ending when clients have received the help they sought or when it is apparent that counselling is no longer helping or when clients wish to end.
>
> If an ending is enforced because the work appears not to be therapeutic, counsellors must make arrangements for care to be taken of the immediate needs of clients in the

event of any sudden and unforeseen endings by the counsellor or breaks to the counselling relationship.

The therapist's holidays and absences for whatever reason are seen
as important in the patient's experience both because the therapist
has inevitably become important and because it is in this area that
the difficulties of the ultimate ending can best be foreseen and
worked through. Counsellors are required to take care to prepare
their clients 'appropriately' for any planned breaks from counselling.
They should take any 'necessary steps to ensure the well-being of
their clients during such breaks'.

These clauses are in addition to the existing codes in that they
recognise the special need for ethical behaviour in relation to
endings. They are welcome in that ending does require awareness
of its specific ethical questions. On the other hand, it is difficult
to legislate for all the potential situations that may arise. Spelling
out some requirements leaves others uncovered and creates more
difficulty in the long run. There are many questions about the judgements implied, especially the decision about when steps need to be
taken and what the 'necessary steps' might be seen to be. The United
Kingdom Council for Psychotherapy has a set of ethical requirements which must be incorporated into the codes of all member
organisations. These codes do not usually mention ending as such,
but all therapists must be aware of the specific problems of ending
therapy in a way that is ethical and must also apply the requirements that are in the existing codes for all their behaviour when
there are no specific requirements for ending.

Conclusion

Ethical behaviour is required of therapists at all times. The ending
process imposes particular strains because in some ways it involves
departures from what is ordinary. By definition it is about change,
and very often it is brought about by change. It demands the most
of therapists in flexibility and willingness to accept what is different,
and mainly of course to accept loss. Even where the therapist seeks
the ending because the work has become impossibly difficult, he or
she must recognise both the loss to the patient of a hope that therapy
could be valuable and also the loss of the narcissistic satisfaction
of achievement. While working with these difficulties and the strong
feelings they arouse, the therapist must still consider the patient's
needs and as far as possible make the ending useful for the patient.

References

Bollas, C. and Sundelson, J. (1995) *The New Informants*, London: Karnac.

Clarkson, P. (1996) *The Bystander*, London: Whurr.

Clarkson, P. and Murdin, L. (1996) 'When rules are not enough: reflections on the spirit of the law in ethical codes', *Counselling* 7 (1): 31–35.

Firestone, R. (1997) *Suicide and the Inner Voice*, London: Sage.

Freud, S. (1914) 'Observations on transference love', *SE* 12: 157.

Kennedy, R. (1998) *The Elusive Human Subject*, London: Free Association Books.

Klimovsky, G., Dupetit, S. and Zysman, S. (1995) 'Ethical and unethical conduct in psychoanalysis', *International Journal of Psycho-analysis* 76: 977.

8

ENDGAME

Last sessions

Every therapy eventually reaches a last session. The ending phase may be a matter of minutes or seconds for the patient who walks out abruptly or it may be as long as a year. The therapist's ending for reasons such as moving away as described in Chapter 5 may also lead to long ending phases. However long the ending is, each therapist will need to decide whether there are specific techniques that are appropriate for the ending phase and what may be the theoretical rationale for any difference that is made. De Simone (1997) considers that in a therapy that has gone reasonably well, there should be no particular problems and no change of technique in the ending phase. Readiness to end will ideally involve a willingness in the patient to negotiate and discuss the ending. The therapist's own feeling that ending now will be all right is another important criterion and will contribute to the possibility that the ending phase will be of value to both.

Change to the sense of time in the ending phase

In order to reach a point at which ending is accepted and even desired, the patient must have changed and so must the therapist. One of the most important and least noted changes is the way in which the sense of time has altered. The sense of time is a candidate to be our sixth sense. It follows self-awareness and yet it is variable and changes as the patient changes. The sense of time varies developmentally, culturally and socially. The patient arrives in therapy with no time to spare or without knowing how to use time. The sessions are treated as precious short stretches of time, or are endless deserts. The end of each session is a deprivation or a punishment. Alternatively, the sessions are grabbed and smashed or crumpled up and the patient cries out for more time, but good time instead of bad.

The therapy session shares in the cultural changes in our attitude to time. Time has been deconstructed in the arts. We have been taught to accept the novel or film that begins with a flashback or a scene in the present which frames a story from the past. We used to need time machines or space travel to explain such time changes, but we have become so accustomed to them that we no longer find such artificial aids necessary. Time travel is an acceptable fiction and of course all therapies are likely to include a certain amount of it. We also know now that what happens in therapy is also a construct. There is a historical past and there are truths that can be verified. Nevertheless, the story that is told to the therapist is bound to be coloured and shaped by the present. As in a film, for example, *The French Lieutenant's Woman*, we see the past from the point of view of the present. In this film, the story is set in the eighteenth century, but it is framed and interspersed with the story of the actors who are playing the parts. Their story echoes and interweaves with the story from the past. The end of the film is in the present when the film within a film has finished. Much the same thing will have happened in therapy. What we need to know is that the story ends in the present. The actors will have been affected both by what happened in the past and the way in which it has been remembered in the course of the therapy, but a good ending needs to be in the present.

The change to an ability to live in the present is one of the main improvements that can be derived from a therapy that is good enough. Living in the present in this sense implies being able to remember the past without letting it dominate thoughts, feelings or patterns of relationships. When people arrive in therapy, they find the past, present and future are all unbearable for one reason or another. For the manic depressive, the future is either greeted with careless insouciance or a depressed certainty that it will be bad. The schizoid may believe that it will be lonely and the paranoid that it will attack with worse strokes of fortune than the present or the past. Getting better in all these cases may mean that the sense of time allows for an awareness of the future, but does not let it overshadow the importance of attention to what is happening now.

Michael Eigen describes the importance of allowing time to move at whatever pace is needed for the moment in a session:

> Let's relax into giving time a chance to develop its own flow, and allow that there should be a 'later' or a 'then',

or enough room or enough of a gap so that some kind of approach of movement from here to there is possible. So that analysis can be possible and develop over time. . . . In this sense you might want to help a person view therapy as a kind of psychic gymnasium, to build up tolerance, at certain times, for just seeing a moment through.

(1997: 114)

'Seeing a moment through' implies being able to allow what is potentially painful to take its course before the customary defences click in. It is above all an experience that is provided by almost any model of psychotherapy for anyone who can tolerate it at all. Therapy has its own time zone. In the postmodern era we are fragmented in many ways, and we recognise to some extent our fragmentation. In therapy, time can stretch or condense. It can speed up or slow down, sometimes achieving the point where rushing on to the next thing may not be necessary.

Therapy is a process that may change the sense of time. In almost all models of psychotherapy, people are seen to present with a disturbance in the sense of the passage of time. There are disturbances also in memory and these imply a difficulty with letting the past go and with living with what there is. There is also often a difficulty in accepting the rate at which time passes. Either it moves too fast, taking away one's time in a persecutory way, or it moves too slowly and each moment is too full in the senses of both being too long and not providing enough. Personal time is variable and elastic and may change dramatically for the patient during the course of therapy, and requires the therapist to have the same experience, moving perhaps from boredom or anxiety to a calmer acceptance of the rate at which time passes. Whereas at the beginning of therapy the fifty-minute hour may seem much too long, a great space to fill, or much too short, never giving enough time to say everything, by the end of therapy, the session, both in itself and as a template for most other stretches of time, may have become more comfortable, with the patient more able to fit it to him and to fit into it.

There is of course value in recognising fragmentation which may in itself imply the ability to change. One of the ways in which patients can be helped to bear whatever pain they have is by gradually developing understanding that whatever there is in the present is not all there is. I can feel or know something different from what I feel or know now. We could call this a sense of something more, something that continues, a core self, or simply a knowledge that the

135

different selves that make up myself will not cease to be available. In any case, there is a change that can take place which allows a greater tolerance of whatever there is.

The paradox of leaving therapy begins to make sense if we see it in the context of both continuity and a tolerance of discontinuity. The present is valued, and a vision of the future that includes separation can be faced, but without undue anxiety. This attitude allows for the stage in which ending becomes part of the discourse that makes up the therapy but is neither dreaded nor desired to an extent that creates unbearable anxiety. The level of anxiety over time is an indicator of whether it is yet time to end.

Time can be conceptualised as a circle in which we always return to the beginning, or an arrow moving only in one direction. Angela Molnos (1995) writes that in the twentieth century we have become more aware of time as an arrow. The image of time's arrow flying in only one direction is a symptom of the anxiety of our age, in which we feel ourselves to be shooting helplessly forward at a frightening speed and with an implication of destruction at the end. Medieval images seem more comfortable in that the closed universe provided a container. The planets moved in closed circles round the sun, and beyond the solar system the stars were safely fixed. Time was conceived as a cycle. Human life followed its destiny and returned to God from whence it came.

In order to end therapy or any relationship in this age, we have to achieve the recognition that time is irreversible: we cannot have the past back, not even in memory, since memory continually makes changes. We have to move forward and that does mean facing the unknown. Therapy may help in the discovery that moving forward need not imply abandonment of the past and of what has been of value in it.

Readiness to end entails willingness to remember and willingness to forget. Time can be allowed to move fast or to slow down. There are observable cycles and yet overall a movement that is forward and irreversible. At the beginning of therapy some patients may have been unable to allow any return to the past. References by the therapist to what happened with the parents are regarded as avoidance of the therapist's own role in the pain and discomfort of the present:

> Ms Y came to see a therapist because she had been raped, and was advised by the police and also a friend whose mother was a therapist that therapy might help her 'to come

to terms with the experience'. She appeared to be very reluctant to talk much about the rape or anything else, but Mr Z, the inexperienced therapist who saw her, thought that she was suffering from post-traumatic stress and that she would soon learn to trust him and tell him more. In fact she never told him much about her history other than that her father had left her mother when she was 5 years old. Occasionally he sent her parcels of completely unsuitable presents. She remembered him sending her a teddy bear when she was 14 and a copy of Chaucer in the original when she was 7. Both of these things could be seen as quirky but perhaps well meaning. She saw them as deliberate attempts to show that he did not care how old she was or what she was like.

Mr Z soon found himself at the sharp end of some very negative transference. His interpretations were met with a stony silence, or loud shouting along the lines that he never understood a word she said and all that he said was unbelievably naive. She had read a great deal about psychology and psychoanalysis herself and was inclined to say, 'If you'd read any Klein at all you'd know better than to say that.' Mr Z had read Klein and was hurt by this constant swarm of stings. 'What would you say if you were me?' he asked. She replied, 'You can't get out of it that easily. That's pathetic escapism.' Mr Z also said, 'You treat my words as if they were unsuitable presents from your father. The difference is that with me you can send them back.' This produced even more fury: 'You think you can talk about my father and that lets you off the hook. You know nothing at all about my father.'

This went on for some time before gradually, with the help of intensive supervision, the therapist fed back the double binds that the patient produced for him. He could not speak of the past and he could not be tolerated as himself in the present. He did, however, survive in the time-honoured way that therapists usually do, by a mixture of empathy, humanity and enough interpretation to keep himself from going mad. Gradually, the barrage of hate and hostility lessened and, with many relapses, some progress was made towards a state in which the therapist himself was tolerated better and was acknowledged to be not totally useless.

Ends of sessions had been particularly difficult times in which Ms Y had fought against the inevitability of the end of the session with various weapons, including refusing to leave and all the gamut of reasons for staying just a few minutes longer. Mr Z had worried greatly about how to deal with this and certainly despaired of being able to end the therapy in a mutual and constructive way. Nevertheless, after five years, Ms Y decided that she wished to train as a psychotherapist; she was already working in an allied profession. To Mr Z's astonishment, she was accepted for training by one of the London organisations and she was told that she would have to change therapists. He was therefore both relieved and chagrined when she told him she intended to finish working with him in six months so that she would have her new therapy in place in order to begin the training.

There was therefore a six-month ending phase in which some of the changes that had been developing in secret were allowed to appear. Mr Z had some inkling that things were not as bad as they had been in her personal or work life, but he had had no idea of the extent to which she had concealed from him her improvement. She said to him about six weeks before they finished: 'you have made a difference to me. I don't know how or what you did, because you never said anything very brilliant, but you seem to have let me feel that I could take my time. Now, I know that I have a lot to learn but there's a lot that I can't tell you. I may not tell anyone or perhaps I may now. I don't know whether I'll be any good as a therapist but I'll be able to have a try at it.' She told him one or two things more about her mother and her memory of her father, but most of the story remained untold in the therapy with Mr Z. They ended with warmth and a sadness that surprised Mr Z, who had at times longed for the ending.

By the process of putting up with an intimate relationship with someone who was very difficult to endure, Mr Z had some-how helped her to be less persecuted both by him and by herself. One of her major changes was the improvement in her ability to use the time available. She had been injured by her father's depar-ture to such an extent that she would never let him repair by giving her presents. Mr Z had somehow managed to repair something by

138

continuing to be there week after week, even though she rejected everything he offered. The desperation at the end of sessions or holiday breaks never disappeared but it diminished as her acceptance of his ordinary, dependable, if not brilliant self enabled her to achieve something like object constancy. Why she chose to train with an organisation that would not accept Mr Z as a training therapist is an interesting question and one that he never fully addressed. What he did say was that it seemed as though she wanted to make clear that he was not very important and could be supplanted by another person, in this case a higher status training therapist. He added that he suspected that she would have wished her father to have been less important to her. She did not greet this with her usual scorn, although she reiterated that of course it was just to do with stupid training requirements and nothing to do with her father. One would hope that the next therapist or analyst was able to make use of the groundwork laid by Mr Z and that good work might have ensued.

Loss and grieving in the ending phase

In this case, the interminability of analysis, as Freud put it, was made very clear. The ending was made less intense because there was very definitely somewhere else to go. There was more emphasis on the future, and the importance of the therapy being ended was to some extent denied. Nevertheless, the sense of time had clearly changed and the last six months became more constructive. Ms Y could not acknowledge the importance of the loss of her father and it could not be evoked. Because so much of the work that is done in therapy relates to losses and the way that we face them, the ending phase provides an opportunity that most people find in no other context to live through an ending that has all the measures of sadness, anger, disappointment, gratitude that go with bereavement and loss in other contexts. These emotions should have been faced before the end, and at the last minute they may be fleeting and easily missed because, if the therapy has gone well, the ending will be a celebration as well as being a loss. The feelings that relate to death and dying may be repressed when the patient is much better and is approaching the end with outward success and perhaps new relationships or a marriage.

The work that has been done on death and dying by Parkes *et al.* is relevant and helpful in considering the processes of ending. Once an ending date is set, the therapist listens for the way in which the patient deals with the inevitability of change and therefore of loss. Birth is a difficult process for the baby, as we all know, but recent thinking implies that the baby may actually be ready to be born. The womb may have become a cramped space. The analogy with therapy is obvious and optimistic. We cannot, however, ignore the analogy with the other end of the life span. Jung emphasised that achieving readiness to die is one of the tasks of adult life. How we make ready is an interesting and difficult problem which each individual will have to solve. All that therapy can do is to provide a context in which the question is raised and there is time to look for an answer.

Nina Coltart is a psychoanalyst who took her own life. This event shocked the analytic world, or at least those parts of it that were not close enough to her to know her mind. On reading her last book *The Baby and the Bathwater* (Coltart 1996) and her interview with Anthony Molino in *Freely Associated* (Molino 1997), one has the opportunity to see how she was prepared for death. Speaking in the context of her study of Buddhism, she wrote:

> Now this of course has considerable impact on what was let's say already an interest of mine; namely the idea of one's own death. If one is not a self, if the ego is a construct, the result of a conditioning, we come to accept, well then, what is there to fear? In any case, it's always been my impression that people fear dying much more than death. . . . But that too hasn't been much sorted out in the West. I mean it does require a lot more contemplation and attention.
>
> (Coltart 1997: 193)

This is far from being a nihilistic view of the self. Coltart also emphasises that meditation is a strenuous process and that an understanding of what is meant by no-self or *anatta* is not acquired quickly or easily. It is certainly not the destruction of the ego (1996: 134). In the same way, the truths that are reached in therapy may enable the individual to end, to face his or her death, but are not quickly or easily available. The Buddha sat under the bodhi tree for seven days and seven nights at a time in order to arrive at some element of enlightenment. For most people, several years of therapy are needed to reach a state in which we can give up and leave behind some of the unwanted aspects of ego.

Coltart herself says that she does not see the Buddha dismissing all aspects of ego as illusion or what Lacan would call *méconnaissance*. As a therapist, she concludes that there is some value in the concepts of true and false self that Winnicott propounded in his paper of 1960, because the true self can allow for stillness at the centre. There is time and space when one reaches this centre for both attention and detachment. I find this view of Winnicott's concept of true self greatly preferable to the wilful unadapted baby that it seems to imply for some.

Coltart found that she could contemplate death as exciting, 'an awfully big adventure' rather than as a terror. She wished to face death consciously, and was only sorry that she would not be able to write a paper about it:

> Mostly I think it will be extremely interesting and it seems to me as if almost the greatest blessing that life can hold is to go consciously into one's own death. It is maddening not to be able to write a paper about it afterwards. But to greet one's death to observe and inspect it would feel like a fitting ending – particularly in a psychotherapist's life.
>
> (1996: 143)

Therapy allows for leaving and parting to be consciously faced. Some patients seek to reduce the frequency of their sessions in order to test their ability to manage without the therapist. Allowing a reduction in the number of sessions per week or month is understandable, but will reduce the intensity of the ending phase and deprives the patient of the most intense and therefore perhaps the most valuable time of loss, of letting someone go with all the anger and sadness that loss entails. On the other hand, a gradual reduction in frequency may enable some patients to face leaving when otherwise they would evade it altogether. If loss is faced, there may be echoes of both birth and death in the experience. In this paradox lies another: the contemplation of birth and death allows both for greater strength in being able to contemplate separation and leads towards a point at which there is less isolation either internally or from the other, although there is separation.

Is there life after death?

We bring ourselves to contemplate ending for a short time, but we revert quickly to optimism and emphasis on the positive. Patients in the ending phase may wish to find manic defences which allow them to believe in new relationships or to deny the ending of the current one. There are often questions, overt or veiled, about the possibility of continuing to see the therapist as a friend or colleague. Trainees do not have to lose contact with their training therapists and analysts in the way that we expect our other patients to manage to do. Therapists vary in the extent of absolute finality in ending. Not many would refuse to allow the possibility of further therapy if it were sought, but most would wish the ending to be final for now.

Becoming a friend or partner is an option that is sometimes taken. Love affairs or sexual relationships with ex-patients are discussed in Chapter 7. Lisa Alther in her novel *Other Women* describes a therapist allowing her former patient to meet her for lunch when they have finished. The patient is delighted, but describes vividly her disappointment at the change from therapist behaviour to behaviour as a friend. The friend says, 'Yes, and I have my problems too,' and does not necessarily wish to listen patiently. These are obvious superficial difficulties. What is much more problematic is the change that this causes to the internalised therapist who is no longer available in the same way as an image or after image. The reality is liable to supervene and remove what went before.

An argument on the side of allowing friendship might be that there is no need for the therapist to seem superhuman. A change to being an ordinary person should not destroy the work that has been done. The aims described in Chapter 1 for almost all analytic therapies imply that therapists would deliberately set out to ensure that they cannot be seen as superhumanly wise or tolerant or restrained. For this reason, many therapists would accept a hug or a handshake at the end of therapy although they might not initiate such a change to physical contact themselves. They would allow themselves to be natural in response, and this does not necessarily invalidate the rigour of what has gone before. It may still be consistent with the wish not to be the one who is supposed to know nor to be adopted as the ideal. A refusal to be idealised is a continuing process or attitude in the therapy. What is likely to be problematic is a sudden change in the final phase of the therapy if a certain amount of idealisation has been tolerated up to that point. Sudden changes are not desirable for a number of reasons. One of the most obvious is that it brings the genuineness and sincerity of the whole therapy into question if the therapist in effect says, 'OK, now we are finishing, you are grown up enough to know that there is no Father Christmas, although I thought it was good for you to believe in him for a while.' Such an attitude to the whole process is clearly likely to be damaging because we are not dealing with children and, although fairy tales have an honoured place in therapy, we are not in the business of telling them as if they were the truth and then recanting later.

The last session

If the therapist is firm about the finality of ending, the patient is faced with a parting and a separation but not with the total loss of the therapist because the therapist can continue to be kept in mind as therapist. Even so, the separation process is bound to bring fear and anxiety insofar as it is experienced as loss. Masud Khan was able to say about his analysis with Winnicott:

> One of the most valuable contributions of DWW's long protective care and coverage over the past twenty years of my growth and development as a person has been that he has changed a catastrophic threat of loss of object into separation anxiety.
>
> (Cooper 1993: 21)

The actual analysis lasted fifteen years, but as fellow members of the British Psycho-analytical Society their relationship continued after the end of formal analysis. For patients who are not colleagues, the ending is different. The patient may panic and wish to change his mind and not part after all. Even when the feelings in the therapeutic couple have reached a point when ending is in view, reverses upset the smooth passage to an ending. This may be the phenomenon known as negative therapeutic reaction which is usually understood to mean that there is anxiety aroused by any improvement of symptoms or state of mind. The anxiety is caused partly by the fear of losing the therapist and partly by much less conscious phenomena described by Sandler *et al.* (1992), and Limentani (1981), for example, as guilt at getting better or envy of the therapist who cannot be allowed the satisfaction of healing. Guilt is caused by the inner voice which demands suffering and exacts continuing reparation.

Whatever the reason for the negative reaction, we all see it happening when there has been a particularly good session or a particularly good therapy which may be about to end. This happens at various points in the process, but is a common experience in the very last session.

143

Mrs AA is a woman of 78 years old. She had Jungian analysis in her twenties and later trained as a counsellor, having had a considerable amount of further therapy of her own. She came to her last therapy because she had experienced what she saw as a series of dreams about her little brother who had died at the age of 5. Both she and her brother had been beaten by the nanny who was looking after them when their mother had died. Her little brother always appeared in the dreams as an innocent child who was helpless in the grip of the cruel woman and was imploring rescue. In the early dreams he was standing on a chair. Mrs AA would interpose herself between him and the woman who was trying to hit him, but she fell down or tripped and was unable to prevent him from being hit while he screamed and cried. The dreams were extremely vivid and distressing. At the same time, Mrs AA, whose husband had died twenty years before, was struggling with a relationship with a man of about her own age, and who wished to come and live with her. She had known him for ten years or so but had never wanted to commit herself to anything more than friendship.

In the course of therapy, which lasted about eighteen months, she explored her feeling of guilt and helplessness over her little brother. She had no children of her own and felt that she was unfit to have been a mother and in fact that she carried the burden of all women who are harmful and destructive to men. With the woman therapist she was able to acknowledge how difficult she found it to allow anyone close to her at all. She had a dry wit and great intelligence and therefore she had many friends, both men and women, but no one was allowed inside the secret garden of her innermost feelings. She was also an artist with a loom, and she could convey a great deal of pain and separation in the images that she wove.

In therapy she could be savage in her attacks, but she was also able to invoke great affection and attachment in the therapist. She was able to allow that she also loved the man she knew, but she could not risk having him come to live in her house. She reached a sort of compromise with this, and decided to end her therapy in the understanding that she had done as much as she could. She agreed with the therapist to have an ending period of about three months. They worked on, dealing with the image of the little boy, seeing in him both the hope and purity of the *puer aeternus* or the eternal child, the saviour, and also the contrary figure of the helpless child. She had seen men as both, and was therefore, not surprisingly, afraid that she could have a great effect, largely damaging, and also that she could have no effect at all on the man who was to be the saviour of the world.

When the last session came, the therapist was very sad in anticipation of ending what she had found to be most illuminating and challenging work. She was also sad that she would not be seeing this brave and lonely woman any more. The session began with Mrs AA saying in great agitation that she had quarrelled with her friend and that he had said he was tired of her prevarication and would not want to come and see her any more. The therapist immediately thought, 'well, we can't end the therapy. She'll be completely on her own and there is obviously much more work to do now.' She waited, however, and on reflection decided that this might be a last-minute panic and that she should persevere with the ending, rather than respond to her own wish to continue to see this patient. She therefore said: 'I know that you are describing a bad quarrel and I don't know whether you will be able to mend it. I also know that we are ending our sessions today and we might both be aware that the end of our meetings is sad and in a sense not to be mended, and yet perhaps there is still something important for you in having the courage to face this final session.' Mrs AA was able to acknowledge in tears that the ending was very important to her and that she would greatly miss the therapist. Nevertheless, she wished to end as they had planned. Her last words were, 'I shall weave something for you and send it so that you will not forget me.' In this way, we could say that she evaded the full force of the ending, and yet, in her sadness and her unprecedented acknowledgement of someone's importance to her, she had faced it as much as anyone does. The therapist heard that she had died within a few months of ending the therapy, so the wall hanging was never finished.

Persisting with the ending when the patient brings an emergency into the last session may not always be the appropriate response, but

145

it is always important to check it in one's own need for the patient and one's own defences against death and the end. Another therapist was faced with a patient whose mother died the day before the last session. This was a sudden, unanticipated death from a stroke. The patient asked whether it would be possible to have more time, and in that case the therapist decided to give another three months to the therapy. The rationale would be that the death of one's mother is a difficult experience to survive for most people. It was not a reparable loss like a quarrel, and it meant that the ending of the therapy could not in any case be fully valued because the patient was in a state of shock. For all these reasons, the change of mind seemed the best choice and in fact the therapy ended on a sad but constructive note at the end of the three months.

Not all therapy ends with sadness. Perhaps a more usual ending would have a celebratory note and would have optimism and energy as the conscious tone. In these cases, the therapist must remember the themes of loss and death. This is usually achieved by making some sort of summary of what has been done and what has not been done. There are bound to be disappointments and areas that have not been touched. The whole journey may have been to an unforeseen destination, and in any case, the person who is arriving is not the same as the person who set out. Both the patient and the therapist will have ideas about what has been missed, although they may be different. Patients can be encouraged to say what they have missed or not been able to change. Therapists are less likely to say what they think has not been done unless it relates to what the patient has already said. To raise something that has not been discussed already as a lack seems cruel, and would be a poor reflection on the work of the therapist. On the other hand, to recapitulate what both agree has not been possible or only marginally achieved is to face as far as possible the reality of the relationship and its shortcomings.

One thing that is often missed by therapists is the importance of the patient's gratitude. We are so used to hearing and acknowledging negative transference that it can be quite difficult to hear and accept genuine gratitude. Yet even a superficial knowledge of Klein suggests that gratitude is the antidote to envy, allowing a person to be at peace with himself and, even more importantly, allowing that another can have something good which may in part be given or shared but which does not have to be destroyed. This in itself implies that the therapist can be left and can be allowed to keep whatever good she still has in the patient's mind. Hinshelwood refers to a patient who spoke in images of planting and growing:

> He knew that getting the sweet peas was connected with my having sweet peas in my front garden. Also, when he was a child there were sweet peas in a wild part of the garden at home, and he loved them, they meant a great deal to him.
>
> (1994: 218)

There may be idealisation in this image, but as Hinshelwood points out, it is connected to the earth and suggests that something may be growing or at least able to grow in the patient. In a last session, such an image of growth can be greeted with hope because, although it may be defensive, it is the patient's last word.

Therapists may also wish to give something to the patient. Melanie Klein, in her account of therapy with Richard (1989), said to him in his last session when he took a drink of water that, since he could not have the good breast, he now wishes to take the good penis of the father into him. The material does not obviously lead to such an interpretation. One might say that it is consistent with her whole pattern of discourse with Richard in which she makes a commentary on all his simple, everyday remarks in terms of her theory of the child's concern with the bodies of the parents and with his own body. Nevertheless, in the context of the last session, she is giving him a gift of the good penis. Will he be able to use a penis that she gives him, or is it an addition, an extra, not his own? Apparently he became a travelling salesman, with a suitcase of objects to display and to offer to others.

This example merely illustrates the uncertain trajectory of all that we offer. We cannot know where it goes or what it might effect. When we are in the endgame, we may be tempted to try to give something extra. It is the last chance, and the patient will no longer be there to repair our sense of ourselves as therapists. Perhaps it is this loss on both sides that leads to the ultimate desire for a return to the real or physical contact at the end. It is a very private moment and we do not know much about what happens, although it is likely that there is often a wish on both sides to express the inexpressible at the last moment.

References

Coltart, N. (1996) *The Baby and the Bathwater*, London: Karnac.
Coltart, N. (1997) 'Interview with Nina Coltart', in Molino, A. (ed.) *Freely Associated*, London: Free Association Books.

Cooper, J. (1993) *Speak of Me as I Am: The Life and Works of Masud Khan*, London: Karnac.

de Simone, G. (1997) *Ending Analysis*, London: Karnac.

Eigen, M. (1997) 'Interview with Michael Eigen', in Molino, A. (ed.) *Freely Associated*, London: Free Association Books.

Hinshelwood, R. (1994) *Clinical Klein*, London: Free Association Books.

Klein, M. (1989) in Steiner, J. (ed.) *The Oedipus Complex Today: Clinical Implications*, London: Karnac.

Limentani, A. (1981) 'On some positive aspects of the negative therapeutic reaction', *International Journal of Psycho-analysis* 62: 379.

Molino, A. (ed.) (1997) *Freely Associated*, London: Free Association Books.

Molnos, A. (1995) *A Question of Time*, London: Karnac.

Parkes, C. M. (1995) *Recovery from Bereavement*, London: Karnac.

Sandler, J., Dare, C. and Holder, A. (1992) *The Patient and the Analyst*, London: Karnac.

Winnicott, D. W. (1960) 'Ego distortion in terms of true and false self', in (1985) *Maturational Processes and the Facilitating Environment*, London: Hogarth.

9

IN MY BEGINNING IS
MY END

The time-limited solution

If it were done when 'tis done, then 't were well
It were done quickly.

(Shakespeare, *Macbeth* I, vii)

How loss is used

Much of this book has been about reconciling the conflicts of
patients and therapists over how long therapy should be. Therapists
in private practice are consciously highly motivated to make therapy
last as long as possible both because their income depends on a
regular number of sessions and because of innate conservatism as
well as resistance to loss. Patients have the opposite motivation. In
most cases, they want to spend as little money and time as possible
in order to leave therapy feeling better and with their lives changed.
These two streams of thought have to meet in making a contract
and in planning an ending. When the contract has a time-limit, the
patient will have to change a great deal in a short time, but paradoxically, the therapist may not have to change as much as in
open-ended work.

In some cases the therapist makes a time-limited contract reluc-
tantly, bowing to practical necessity. Working for agencies, many
therapists have accepted that six or twelve sessions is what the
agency offers or can afford and that if they wish to work for
the agency they must keep within the time-limit. In some cases,
they would prefer to be seeing the patient for longer if they could.
Research has indicated, however, that gain in reported improvement
continues with increased length of therapy only up to twenty-six
sessions. After that the gains reduce until the longest therapies show
little if any continued gain (Howard *et al.* 1986). A study comparing
eight sessions with sixteen found that only very disturbed patients

benefited more from sixteen sessions than from eight (Shapiro 1995). There is therefore good reason to regard time-limited therapy as a treatment of choice in many cases. Therapists have been inclined to see long-term work as their treatment of choice, and it is often necessary to educate the therapist into believing that much can be achieved with specialist training and supervision for the shorter periods of therapy. There is now some excellent training in time-limited psychotherapy.

The most obvious advantage of time-limited work is that both patient and therapist know exactly how much time there is and can adapt their pace accordingly. Time-limited contracts are not necessarily very brief. Although they may be as little as one or two sessions, they may equally be for a year or two years. The end is built into the contract and there is no way that the loss can be avoided or denied if the contract is followed rigorously. There are of course various models of time-limited work and the more cognitive models may be less inclined to deal with the ending of the work overtly. For example, a systemic model of six sessions involves bringing up the idea of ending in the fourth session. The patient is reminded that there are two more sessions and the question of further work to continue or extend what has been done is raised. At this point further referrals may be made or lists of appropriate agencies, including perhaps those for long-term therapy, may be offered. The end of the current work is clearly set out in front of the patient, although feelings about it may not be directly addressed unless the patient shows distress or raises the ending as a problem. In the last session, the patient will be invited to say what has been achieved by the therapy and what has been missed. This will often lead to an opportunity for the patient to speak about the feelings aroused by ending although, again, the therapist will not directly ask about feelings. The emphasis will be on what the patient will do next and how the improvements achieved may be maintained. In a systemic or cognitive model the therapist can stay with known and tested techniques and schemas and may not need to seek resolution through his own change.

In a more psychodynamic or analytic approach, the patient's transferred feelings about the potential loss of the therapist and the therapy may be more directly raised by the therapist. This has to be done carefully, because a danger in time-limited work is that the patient uncovers feelings and memories which are transferred to the therapeutic context and are so profound or disturbing that they cannot be processed or resolved in the time available. Many therapists who have trained in open-ended psychodynamic therapy will find that they think in terms of what is being transferred from the past and what part they find themselves playing for the patient, but will use a great deal of skill in not opening up too many old wounds that cannot be healed in the time that remains.

Mohammed and Smith describe their work for the Women's Therapy Centre as 'neither psychoanalysis nor counselling although it contains elements of both' (1997: 112). They make use of David Malan's three-pointed approach to psychodynamic work to achieve insight by linking accounts of past relationships with the present outside the therapy and the present in the room with the therapist (Malan 1979). If these three points can be linked during the therapy, which is commonly a contract of twelve weeks, the ending may be experienced with acceptance rather than a sense of persecution. Mohammed and Smith have found, like most others in the field, that there is often a crisis in the last few weeks of such a contract, and this crisis raises the whole question of whether there can be any autonomy and self-confidence without the therapist and the therapy, but, by surviving this moment, the patient can gain hope and belief in himself. The therapist must keep faith at this point and not change the ending date, because that would imply doubt.

The therapist is not the only one in the room who thinks differently because of the time-limit. The patient also knows both consciously and at a deeper level that there is just so much time to use. The therapist reinforces this by reminding the patient of how much time there is left and encouraging the patient to think actively about how to use that time. Outcome studies by the Westminster Pastoral Foundation's time-limited project in Counselling in Companies indicate that patients report surprisingly great improvement in just six sessions and one explanation for this is that there is a self-regulatory mechanism in the psyche which enables the patient in most cases to avoid too much regression and to use the time in therapy to change patterns of behaviour, with the reinforcement and encouragement of the therapist acting as catalyst.

Davanloo (1980) is a charismatic therapist who works in a model which depends greatly on his own powerful personality. He makes a judgement about who can use his approach and then breaks down resistance and defence by persistent questioning in which the patient is allowed no escape. He insists on knowing exactly what the counter-productive behaviour is, when it happens and how it happens, and the patient is allowed no avoidance, no hiding-place. He forces the patient to become aware of strong feelings in the present which cannot be avoided, because Davanloo will not let them be concealed. He achieves his aims, or the aims of the patient, by means of connecting the powerful feelings that arise to a sense of discovery, so that the patient is aware that he or she can change and behave differently from the way he or she has behaved before. He sets up an expectation that change can be exciting and liberating. In other words, he enables the patient to see that time's arrow may be moving towards the achievement of goals and strongly suggests that this need not be feared.

One of the most important elements of the therapist's work when it is short term is the warmth and concern that is conveyed by the voice and attitude of the therapist so that the patient knows that the challenging is for his or her own good. Molnos (1995) refers to the healing anger that the patient experiences when the resistance is challenged to such an extent that there is nowhere left to hide. At the moment when the patient is able to be angry at the pressure, and the laying bare of the defence, he or she is able to be free of the defence. Compliance and pleasing the therapist are no longer possible, and although what is experienced is anger that relates to all the compliance and acceptance of the past, the anger itself is nevertheless a moment of separateness in which the patient is free from his or her neurosis and is able to contemplate a less dependent existence.

Davanloo's approach is in some ways very authoritarian, but Molnos (1995) argues that part of its beneficial effect is that it enables the patient to be separate and to experience not needing to be so defensive. Davanloo generally works in only one or two sessions (although he has also worked for up to twenty sessions), and carefully monitors the extent to which the patient can survive his challenge. Most therapists will be less challenging than he is but we can perhaps see a similar rationale for other forms of brief therapy. The therapist can set up a dependency if she is seeking admiration for her wisdom or is too inclined to enjoy being idealised. There would be some danger in such a therapist using the reminders of the approaching ending to tantalise the patient, to say in effect 'aren't you sorry that you have only two more sessions with me?' The implication of speaking of ending is the possibility of independence: 'We have only two more sessions and you will be able to use the time to develop tools for yourself that you can use on your own without me.'

In 'Mourning and melancholia' (1917), Freud wrote of the difficulty of losing someone through death or other means. In one of his most memorable pieces of writing he said that 'the shadow of the object falls upon the ego'. He was speaking of the way in which, through depression, the sufferer feels worthless and treats himself as the useless, powerless one, because the alternative would be to think this of the dead person. Therapists have to be aware that they can become in fantasy the lost person whose shadow falls upon the patient's ego and disables it. There is particular danger of this in long-term therapy, but in short-term work the therapist risks this happening if he is too brilliant and charismatic and allows the patient to see him as the one who knows. Davanloo, for example, guards against this to some extent by using Socratic questioning. The patient must find his own solution, although he is brought to the necessity of finding something by the persistence with which Davanloo pursues him into his avoidance and delays.

Ending: do we really mean it?

One of the most painful questions facing therapists in time-limited work arises when a patient wishes to continue beyond the time-limited contract. Most of the agencies who provide this kind of therapy have strict rules prohibiting therapists from seeing patients after the end of the contract. Like marriage after therapy, however, the continuation of the work is not always seen as impossible. Many GP practices have counsellors or therapists working for them who may choose to see some patients for open-ended contracts or in some cases may take patients into private practice if the patient is willing and they wish to do so. There are obvious arguments for and against these continuations. The therapeutic argument will be that the patient has begun to uncover some part of himself or his past which is now raw and open and must be given more attention before it festers. The therapist will be experiencing the counter-transference effects of being loved and possibly idealised in the transference, even though the time together may have been short.

Clearly, therapists in such a situation need to search themselves and their own motivation carefully. There is likely to be some sort of particular attraction in this patient which relaters to a son/daughter or mother/father transference for the therapist. These Oedipal connections will make it very difficult to let the patient go. No doubt they will affect the extent to which both the patient and therapist wish to continue beyond the contract but they may not make a sound basis for deciding to ignore the contract and postpone the ending. At the very least, they mean that the ending that was agreed in the contract should be carried out and that if work is to be resumed it must be under a new contract. An understanding that there will be a new contract does remove from the patient the experience of letting go of a person who is valued. There is some Oedipal triumph in managing to seduce your therapist into continuing to work with you, and although this may not necessarily be a bad thing, it needs to be recognised. Developmentally, the adolescent seeks to have the parent all to himself, but needs to fail and be compelled to seek relationships of his own. Clearly, this aspect of continuing therapy can be recognised and used.

Ending from the beginning

Because the patient knows that there will be an ending at a specific time as the distinguishing feature of time-limited work, he is unlikely to stay in a childlike state of timelessness, but always seeks to be in a more adult mode with awareness of what is happening to him. This very awareness is part of maturity and is presupposed by the therapist to be possible. If it is not, then time-limited work is contra-indicated, as are some other forms of psychological therapy. If the patient is not able to think or speak articulately, talking therapies are not likely to be able to help unless there is time for the patient to learn to use the therapist. Long-term therapy can allow for regression to some aspects of childhood, but time-limited work requires thinking from the beginning.

Patients who seek time-limited work are achieving the safety of knowing that work will be done at the conscious level. Whatever is going on beneath the surface, something will happen that can be known and understood. There will be an ending, and we can be sure of that at least if nothing else. On the other hand, they are missing out on the middle stage of therapy. John Rowan (1997) writes:

> It seems to me that brief counselling or therapy ignores the middle phase and in effect cheats the patients of the potential hidden within their crisis. It sticks to the easy part where some immediate results can be seen and ignores the more demanding parts where there may be difficulties with the therapeutic relationship itself. It is in the second phase that higher levels of skill and deeper levels of self knowledge are called for on the part of the counsellor.
>
> (1997: 193)

The second stage to which Rowan is referring is the middle part of the therapeutic process. He describes the beginning as dealing with the presenting problems or symptoms. The second phase is entered when these initial difficulties have been removed and the patient begins to look more deeply at the causes of the problems and the repeating patterns they have made in the past, perhaps from childhood. Time-limited work is not intended to upset deeply held convictions about childhood or other aspects of life unless that is essential to deal with the present. An adult finishing time-limited work may have solved an immediate problem and may have acquired tools for the future but will not usually have faced fully the fear and anxiety of childhood.

The third phase of time-limited work involves applying the learning of the second phase to the everyday life of the present. These phases in practice are often blurred and overlapping. Nevertheless, Rowan makes clear that the patient who has to move straight from dealing with the presenting problem into the ending does miss an opportunity. In analytic work, the opportunity that is missed is the possibility of entering the time of childhood where one can just mess about with no specific aim or end in view. Such apparent idleness does have a purpose. There is a risk of boredom and anxiety but it can also achieve changes at a fundamental level, as a reading of Winnicott's clinical work shows.

Something is lost and something gained which ever mode of work is chosen. One thing is very clear: in time-limited work, the therapist must be prepared to work for an ending right from the beginning and must not waver in the view that an ending is desirable. Time-limited work requires the therapist to be much more active in technique, even if not as active as Davanloo, for example. Feltham (1997) lists some questions that the therapist should ask after a session:

- Have I generally established a sense of urgency, expectation and hope?
- In this session did I sensitively apply a degree of temporal pressure?
- Exactly what did I do in this session that helped to move matters forward?
- Did I at any time inappropriately hurry or pressurise the patient?

(1997: 139)

To these, I would add

- Did I remind the patient of just how much time there is left before the ending?

One aim of the therapist in reminding the patient of the ending is to prevent aimless dawdling. The patient has set himself a goal and the therapist's job is to help him to move towards it. Of course the goal may be changed, but there will have to be a replacement goal. Sometimes the goal may be to find a goal, but that can then be delineated as the very important need to discover what the patient wants. Because of this pressure, the ending of such problem-solving work is bound to relate to the problem. There will be an element of success or failure that may be tackled less punitively because of the effect of the therapy, but will still be part of the atmosphere of the ending. Sometimes, the main achievement of a patient is to be able to forgive him- or herself and the therapist for not having achieved the goal that was set or for achieving it only partially.

Therapists have taken varying positions about the need to specify the ending date in time-limited work. One approach is to offer up to six sessions and allow the patient to decide what number will be best. This gives the patient complete control but does not always allow sufficiently for deference and feelings such as: 'You must have to see many people who are much worse than me.' Some therapists say that there will be six sessions in total, but allow for them to be spread over varying intervals according to the progress that is made and the type of problem brought. In this model, the amount of contact is known and agreed but the final ending date is not known. Mann (1979), on the other hand, is very clear that in his twelve-session model, the date of the final session will be set in the initial contract and will not be varied. He is telling his patients that he is confident that they will be ready to go by then. This approach emphasises the extent to which the time-limited model shows the necessity for action and for change. Loss is inherent from the beginning, but 'The stimulus of loss makes all possession mean' (Emily Dickinson).

The stimulus of loss may also bring to the forefront feelings of being displaced, jealousy of patients who will follow, anger with the therapist who gives just so much and then disappears. These sorts of feelings may be painfully aroused but may be dealt with only indirectly as part of the presenting problem. The therapist may be aware of the deeper significance, particularly in terms of the relationship between patient and therapist, but will keep such thoughts to himself. Psychoanalytic interpretations will be made only if absolutely essential to remove a block that is preventing dealing with the present task.

From the therapist's point of view, restraint is essential. He must not draw feelings towards himself because he must not make the ending more difficult. Taking into account the possibility of sometimes ending therapy that has not achieved its agreed goal, the therapist also has to be prepared for some disappointment. Analytic therapists are particularly likely to feel dissatisfied because they have rightly resisted the temptation to encourage transference. There will usually be other achievements to outweigh this frustration. There may sometimes be minimal achievement or none that can be recognised. Of course it often happens that the patient who achieves little was not well motivated in the first place.

One of the causes of failure is the patient's lack of motivation; for example, if he attends therapy only because he has been sent by an employer, partner, etc. Without the desire to make changes for himself, the patient is likely to go away much the same, and the end of the therapy is likely to be half-hearted and full of 'not much'. The patient who finds good reason to want to change and has the courage to see that he or she needs to change, and does not simply wait for the rest of the world to change first, is likely to participate in the high success rate reported by Feltham (1997: 140), who quotes a study showing that 53 per cent of patients reported improvement by the eighth session and 90 per cent by the 104th session. Outcome studies show results to be as good for short-term therapy as for long-term therapy. The benefit that is attained after a hundred sessions seems to be increased self-understanding or in the continuing support of a therapist rather in improvement to symptoms or problems.

Some endings in brief therapy can be startling in the extent of improvement that is reported:

> Ms BB is a woman aged 23. She came to a GP surgery counsellor reporting panic attacks and seemed listless and uninterested in anything. She had a small child of 3 whom she barely mentioned, except as a nuisance to be palmed off on someone else if possible. She had a partner who was reported as neglectful, often out in the evening and not willing to help with the child during the day, even though he was unemployed. Ms BB herself was very attached to her mother and said that she would like to take a graphics design course but could not leave her mum as she would have to do if she were to travel to the nearby town to take the course.

157

In the six sessions that were agreed, Ms BB came to life. The therapist showed little interest in the panic attacks but concentrated on the focus suggested by the patient that she would like to be able to enrol in the graphic design course that might lead to a job. The patient was able to express her anger with both her mother and her partner and to plan what she needed to say to each one. She discovered that her panic attacks took place when she was out shopping with her mother and related to becoming like her mother with no life of her own.

As a result of facing her difficulties and finding ways of talking about them, she found that she was able to take more of an interest in her little daughter. She arranged for childcare and discovered that her mother could actually do without her. She enrolled for the course. All went so well that the therapist's concern became: 'is this too good to be true?' The improvement was maintained however, and in the last session the therapist decided to voice her anxiety that difficulties were being kept hidden. The patient showed some relief at this and said that she was afraid to seem ungrateful but she was anxious about how well she would be able to manage the requirements of the course in graphic design. Between them, they were able to establish that Ms BB should be allowed to do her best, even if that did not always bring success. The therapist was reassured by this element of real anxiety and in the follow-up session six months later found that the improvement had continued.

Such improvement as this is by no means rare, although of course we suffer from the lack of any way of controlling for the comparative effects of other possible models or lengths of therapy. In the absence of research that can look at differential outcomes for one individual, we have to accept provisionally that working with a time-limit and hence an ending in view is beneficial for most people. Nevertheless, it is very different in kind from the long dialogue with another mind that is possible in long-term analytic work and to make a comparison is hardly comparing like with like. For the moment we can be thankful that both kinds of work still exist, and that endings must play an important role in any kind of therapy.

References

Davanloo, H. (1980) *Short Term Dynamic Psychotherapy*, New York: Aronson.

Feltham, C. (1997) *Time-limited Counselling*, London: Sage.

Freud, S. (1917) 'Mourning and melancholia', *SE* 14.

Howard, K., Kopta, S., Krause, M. and Orlinsky, D. (1986) 'The dose–effect relationship in psychotherapy', *American Journal of Psychiatry* 146: 775.

Malan, D. (1979) *Individual Psychotherapy and the Science of Psychodynamics*, London: Butterworth.

Mann, J. (1979) *Time-limited Psychotherapy*, Cambridge, MA: Harvard University Press.

Mohammed, C. and Smith, R. (1997) 'Time-limited psychotherapy', in Lawrence, M. and Maguire, M. (eds) *Psychotherapy with Women*, London: Macmillan.

Molnos, A. (1995) *A Question of Time*, London: Karnac.

Rowan, J. (1997) 'Transpersonal therapy', in Feltham, C. (ed.) *Which Psychotherapy?*, London: Sage.

Shapiro, D. (1995) 'Finding out how psychotherapies help people change', *Psychotherapy Research* 5 (1).

10

ENDINGS IN TRAINING AND SUPERVISION

Endings in training

Training in psychotherapy must vary according to the model and modality being taught. Traditionally, the model has been something like an apprenticeship, and something like an initiation. Recently there has been a strong movement to make psychotherapy into a profession, and this has resulted in codes of ethics and practice and in training requirements. Most training in analytic psychotherapy is designed to encourage long-term or open-ended work. Trainees are required to have personal therapy of the appropriate kind for the duration of the course and do not end with their own therapy, unless something goes wrong, until after they have finished training. They may think that training is interminable and wish for it to end, but the effect of training is to make the ending of the work into an idea but not a reality.

The traditional requirements for training in psychoanalytic psychotherapy, analytical psychology or psychoanalysis go something like this:

All candidates must see as a minimum:

- one patient three to five times a week for two years;
- one patient two to five times a week for eighteen months.

After the second training patient has been seen for long enough, the final paper may be written with the supervisor's approval. Everything depends on being able to see two patients for the required length of time, and of course doing so in a way that the supervisor can approve. Most training requires two individual supervisors, one for each patient, so that two ways of working are experienced and also so that assessment is not restricted to one person's viewpoint.

Counselling training on the other hand is much more likely to have requirements in terms of numbers of hours. Thus the British

Association for Counselling requires 450 hours of supervised case work as a minimum to be completed before a counsellor may seek accreditation. Many other training organisations have chosen a middle path between the two, with some requirements being stated in terms of hours and some in terms of numbers of patients seen.

We can easily see the difficulties that the training organisations face. How can you tell that someone has done enough work to be able to use their experience constructively? How can you assess someone unless they have done a good deal of the kind of work that they are training to do? Training in long-term psychoanalytic work clearly requires that trainees should have worked in at least the middle stage of analytic work so that the transference has been faced in various forms and the candidate has shown ability to tackle whatever the two patients bring. At the other end of the spectrum, many counsellors are increasingly likely to do only short-term work and they need experience of that. They will therefore experience many endings but may be able to avoid the pain and anguish of these more frequent endings and also their value in therapy.

All training needs to be clear about the reasons for the amount of experience required of trainees. The current lack of statutory regulation of counselling, psychotherapy and psychoanalysis means that trainees reach the end of their training and qualify with very different levels of experience behind them. Deciding how much training is enough is done by individual training committees or, increasingly often, by university committees.

The thoroughness and therefore the volume of case work needed in a training seems to me to be determined by the difficulty and responsibility of the undertaking. All those who work in this field are likely to be in a position to do good and therefore also to do harm. They may be influencing people's lives for better or for worse. There seems to me to be no excuse for a training that ends after a brief encounter with clients or patients. No training in counselling or psychotherapy should, in my view, allow people to finish until they have studied a theoretical rationale and worked satisfactorily with clients or patients for at least four years part-time with concurrent personal therapy.

Length is essential in training because the theory must not just be learned but must be assimilated thoroughly through supervision of practice. The nature of the practice, on the other hand, may well need to depend on the kind of work that will eventually be done. Teachers have a duty to ensure that the training is fitted to the work. Thus a counselling training should logically ensure that it includes the skills of brief work, and if its trainees are not being required to include long-term cases in order to qualify, they must be aware that they are qualified only to specialise in short-term work and to refer on for long-term work. A training that equips someone to work in all temporal modalities is necessarily long and arduous and not everyone would wish to do that. On the other hand, everyone needs to be clear about what they are trained and equipped to do. This is vital for the ethics and professional standards of both counselling and psychotherapy.

Endings are problematic for training in all areas of counselling and psychotherapy. In Chapter 9, I examined the importance of endings in time-limited work. Although time-limited work requires great skill it does have schemas, particularly in systemic and cognitive approaches which can be taught and learned. Trainees can develop micro-skills which will enable them to work within the time pressures of a six- or twelve-session model and to make constructive use of those pressures. If a training does genuinely teach people to work in this way, it is bound to address the matter of endings, probably by means of exercises and role play and also by supervision of case work in which endings will occur.

In analytic psychotherapy training there is a greater problem. Trainees are specifically required to carry out ongoing long-term work and will hope not to have to deal with an ending in their training cases. A difficulty that supervisors will have to address is the tendency of trainees to practise defensively and to collude with patients because of their anxiety not to lose a training case. Thomas Freeman wrote about the projections that arise in the trainee's view of the patient who is wanted and needed and takes the place therefore of a parent who had to be pleased, mollified and reassured (1991: 204). Freeman makes the provocative suggestion that there is an advantage in having the analysis and supervision done by the same person so that such projections can be recognised and understood at depth as part of the analysis. This would be a very controversial view because it risks confusing the management of the patient with the transference to the analyst. Freeman is in any case speaking pragmatically of the situation in Northern Ireland where there was a shortage of possible analysts and supervisors.

Nevertheless, if future practice is to be in the profound and moving long-term work that is being supervised, ending cannot be addressed except from the supervisor's challenge to collusive tendencies and from other contexts such as the personal experience of the candidate or through reading the theory. Many trainees are

162

experienced workers, perhaps already qualified counsellors, and will have other supervision where ending may well be addressed. There is some research that has shown that outcomes as reported by clients are not affected by whether or not the therapist is a trainee or by whether or not the therapist approved of the timing of the ending (Macdonald: 1992). Perhaps the patient will make an ending anyway if he needs to do so.

One of the most difficult tasks for a training supervisor and for the organisation is the assessment of patients before they are seen by trainees. The trainees provide a valuable service in that they work with their patients with great energy and devotion. They are having the most minute and detailed supervision that is ever given, in that each patient is individually supervised once a week. The trainees are encountering theory for the first time and are thinking about and discussing it continuously. They have faith and commitment and are also in the middle of their own therapy. For this reason too, they provide patients with the best that they can possibly give as long as they are consistently challenged over the need to placate. For all these reasons, one could argue that patients are gaining a great deal if they are accepted into a training scheme.

On the other hand, patients are assessed for, among other things, their staying power. To benefit from the work, the patient needs to be willing to stay for at least two years. What may not be said in so many words, but is usually clear to both parties, is that this length of stay is needed for the trainee as well as for the patient. The temptation that the patient may or may not avoid from then on is to use the threat of leaving. The patient will suspect that the one thing his therapist least wants is for him to leave. The trouble for both is that this is of course true. Some training courses will send a trainee back to begin again if a patient leaves after twenty-three months. Such a requirement will exacerbate the difficulty with ending and most of the training bodies are, in practice, willing to consider a case on its merits. Because of the reality of the disaster that stringent application of the requirement could imply for a trainee, he or she is least likely to be able to address the possibility of ending in a way that makes it a constructive part of the work. Yet that above all is what the patient needs.

In counselling training the difficulty with ending may lie in the opposite direction with the trainee's inability to address the client's wish to end at a time that seems premature. In any profession, trainees are likely to be tentative, and in counselling there is a strong tendency to value the client's ability to decide what is right for himself. Without denying this ability and right to decide, the psycho-dynamic school would be likely to urge the trainee to pause long enough to discover whether the client has hidden from himself an anxiety which could be eased by understanding it in the counselling relationship. Supervisors have the difficult task of helping trainees to work with balancing a necessary scepticism about readiness to end with a willingness to end well if that is what the client is determined to do.

A clear contract at the beginning needs to include the overt information that the trainee is on a training course. If this is made clear, the patient's temptation to use the power that this gives may be overtly addressed. It may well echo the power that the child tried to find to attack parents who seemed all powerful. It may be a more subtle wish for revenge on the parent who did not seem to be powerful enough. The child in the patient wishes the therapist to be the one who is supposed to know and the one who is powerful enough to make everything safe. All therapists will be familiar with the testing that goes on in the early stages of therapy to discover whether the therapist can cope with what the patient needs to bring. This testing will often include challenging the boundaries of time and sometimes space. Therapists are well used to having to manage and interpret infringements of the expected timekeeping and sometimes the keeping to the appropriate space. Part of the skill of the work is to decide when and how to take up these infringements and how firmly to make the framework of the therapy clear and inviolable.

A trainee has the added task of taking up, and at some point addressing, the patient's fear that she does not have sufficient skill or knowledge to deal with what the patient believes are uniquely appalling problems. This fear may be expressed in any of the ways in which ending is used as a threat. The threat is usually well concealed behind the rational problems of the external world: 'I will have to leave in a few months because I am beginning a new job/course/relationship, etc.' Or 'I have to leave because I cannot afford the fees.' The first group of reasons relates to the patient achieving power and status and may be thought about in terms of what cannot be entrusted to the therapist but must be assumed by the patient for himself. Such premature independence is often a defence against the suffering of loss. Some loss may confront the trainee therapist and will have to be endured, even though it is particularly difficult to face the loss of a patient when the trainee's own therapy has not yet reached the ending stage.

Patients are afraid of being held in therapy for ever and the trainee therapist has to reach the internal conviction that the patient may leave and that will not be the end of the world. If this cannot be achieved the patient may feel too much needed, and this will often resurrect conflicts with needy parents.

The second group of reasons related to money and time for therapy connects with what the patient is willing to give the therapist. Again, this is not unique to training therapy but in that context has a particular relevance to the patient's fear that he is being seen only because the trainee needs a training patient. This fear leads to defence and resistance connected with what can be given to the therapist. The patient in effect is saying, 'I am already giving you too much and will not give you any more.' This is as useful as any other information that the patient gives about his greatest fears. If the therapist feels secure enough about being a trainee, attacks on this front can be used, even though they have the difficulty of being based in knowledge of the therapist's actual situation.

The trainee's ability to work with such feeling in the patient will certainly be affected by his or her confidence that being a trainee can be discussed. It is not a shameful secret that needs to remain hidden if possible. Macdonald's research is an example of a study which shows that trainees have outcomes that are as good as those of more experienced therapists (1992). The trainee needs to face her narcissistic need to be successful immediately and with this patient, and then to put it behind her enough to accept that if that cannot be achieved and more time is needed, then so be it. This inner freedom is essential if the patient is to be free to choose to either go or stay. If this kind of freedom can be achieved, the patient may be helped to become aware of all the envy of the parents' satisfaction from having him as their child. Parents certainly get a great deal out of being parents in most cases, and therapists get a great deal out of being therapists, both in terms of learning and in terms of satisfaction. Why should the trainee not get something out of seeing this patient? Likewise, why should the patient not envy the trainee for the training, and for the satisfaction and achievement that it might bring?

Patients who are ambivalent are likely to find all sorts of reasons to leave. Faced with an ambivalent patient who is complaining, for example, about the fee, a trainee may be tempted to comply and reduce it to a point at which he becomes resentful of the patient. This is obviously counter-productive. Some reduction may be reasonable because trainees are likely to be seeing people who do not have much income. On the other hand, Symington (1986) discovered that his patient benefited when he realised that the low fee he was charging her represented his low expectations and even lower opinion of her. He understood then that the patient needed higher expectations in order to achieve more. In fact, he discovered that she was already capable of more than he had thought possible. Trainees need to have high expectations of their patients and to expect patients to have high expectations of the therapist too. This does not mean being unrealistic about fees. There are times when a reduction is possible and does enable someone to stay in therapy when necessary. Both patient and therapist may need to achieve a state in which they have higher hopes of each other.

Trainees have to end their own personal training therapy. Some choose to go on long after they have finished the training. Others leave at the first available moment when the training requirements are completed. Training committees have no jurisdiction over this choice and it is usually thought to be the trainee's own business. There are, however, unique difficulties to negotiate in that ex-therapists may become colleagues, and this will have to be negoti-ated as a future possibility during the ending phase. This may add to the difficulty of ending, often as much for the therapist as for the trainee. On the other hand, some trainees may have been in therapy for many years and have reached a natural stopping place before the end of a long training, and might benefit from experiencing an ending. Those who are able to stop therapy very precipitously at the end of training raise some questions about the value of what they have been doing before, although there may be practical reasons to end soon. There may be financial difficulties, as training often necessitates taking out loans. If this is the case, the ending may well have been planned before the actual qualification takes place. For those who are not in such urgent need to stop, the value of a con-sidered ending needs to be taken into account.

Ending supervision

For trainees even more than for other therapists, supervision is a vital part of the work. Trainees learn both from what the supervisor says and from what the supervisor does. That is why supervision may be the only place in which trainees can think constructively about endings; it can also be the only place in which they can hear about the way in which an experienced therapist thinks about endings. The supervisor is also a role model and can demonstrate his or her own attitude to contract making and to the opening up of the ending process. Supervision, like therapy, has to reach its own ending in due course. Like everyone else, supervisors have to struggle with their own resistance to endings.

The supervisor of a trainee has a double problem when a patient wishes to end therapy, in that he or she is likely to prefer the trainee's work to continue smoothly if it is intended to be open-ended and will also wish the trainee to have the opportunity to succeed in the training. The supervisor's concern to demonstrate professional competence is somewhere in the background too. If the supervisor presides over the sudden departure of a training patient, does that not in some way reflect on the skill and experience of the supervisor? Some people might think so.

In any case, the patient's struggle to bring to the session his or her wish to leave is likely to be difficult for the supervisor to hear as well as for the trainee:

> Ms CC had been assessed as a patient for a training therapy scheme. She was a student taking a course in fine art and had little money. She came from a family background in which her mother had been schizophrenic and had eventually killed herself. Her father had left the home and she had been brought up by her aunt and uncle. She was articulate and had read a considerable amount of psychology and self-help literature. She was strongly motivated and had friends who were in therapy. She had a conflictual but three-year-long relationship with a male partner. Although she had a very disturbed background, she was thought to be sufficiently motivated and psychologically minded to be a suitable training patient.
>
> She was allocated to Mrs DD, who met her for four sessions. In this time Ms CC was rather withdrawn and, although she told something of her history, Mrs DD found it very difficult to make contact with her. The supervisor was expecting some difficulties to arise in the transfer from the assessing therapist, and encouraged interpretations about the problem of having to make do with an aunt when one would rather have one's mother. What was not said was that the mother was not to be relied upon. After the fourth session, the patient wrote to the therapist saying that she had not felt comfortable at all with the therapist and would not be returning.

The therapist was taken by surprise, and was very upset that there was to be no opportunity to put right or repair what might be wrong. She telephoned the patient and said that she thought the patient should come back to discuss her difficulties in another session. The patient responded angrily that she had already made up her mind and would not return.

The trainee then told her supervisor what had happened. The supervisor's first response was anger. Why had the trainee not been able to get the patient back, and why had she not waited until after supervision to make a move? The telephone call seemed hurried and ill advised. She was rather brusque with the trainee, who burst into tears, saying that she had done the best she could but had felt a great sense of urgency to get something done before supervision. Both the trainee and the supervisor then began to look at the parallel processes that were involved. The trainee was feeling like leaving the supervisor. She had clearly been experiencing some of the same feelings as the patient, in that both were afraid of the unpredictable and terrifying mother who would have no ability to understand feelings of fear or inadequacy but would snap destructively at any weakness shown.

There was no possibility at this stage of reviving the therapeutic relationship, but the trainee and supervisor were able to deepen and develop their own relationship because some of the inevitable fears that go with training and assessment were exposed and expressed. They were also able to discuss the question of how to deal with a sudden ending or, more usefully, with talk of an ending.

In the case described above, the supervisor managed to recognise her own part in the difficulties that the trainee was experiencing. She had been angry and had felt that the trainee should have done better. This might be true, but it is a judgement that needs to be mediated by an attitude of shared responsibility. The supervisor might well have been angry with herself and displaced her anger on to the trainee. After all, the supervisor had not seen and pointed out the patient's terror of the therapist's power to be like her mother.

Supervisors can be powerful and terrifying to trainees and need to recognise the responsibility that goes with power. In the training situation it is tempting for trainees and supervisors to set up a collusive atmosphere in which everything that is difficult is caused by the patient's pathology. Sometimes the supervisor blames the trainee's pathology for anything that goes wrong, and although, of course, this may sometimes be the source of problems, the supervisor is often slow to recognise the extent to which problems tend to echo up and down from patient to supervisor. A balanced view that takes external reality for the patient into account as well as the pathology of all three – patient, therapist and supervisor – is never easy to achieve. The supervisory relationship is likely to encounter its own difficulties and, if it is to reach any depth and value, both supervisor and trainee will have to work through some troubles and disagreements before the trainee can qualify or the relationship can end.

Stoltenberg and Delworth (1987) have a developmental model of the process of supervision in which they describe the supervisee as passing through stages from narcissism to independence or mature dependency.

In Stage 1 the trainee focuses mainly on himself and is motivated by anxiety to perform well. The supervisor's comments are likely to be taken too literally and are not subjected to sufficient internal processing. The main concern is 'How am I doing?' At this stage the supervisor is tempted to be the charismatic one who knows all the answers. She is required to work with this idealisation both of herself and of the process of therapy, as is the therapist for the narcissistic patient. At the second stage or 'level' of Stoltenberg and Delworth's model, the trainee becomes more doubtful both about the supervisor and about the possibility for therapy to solve all difficulties. Patients have not always responded well, and the trainee has many storms to weather. Finally, the trainee may move on to a more independent stage in which he judges his own competence more accurately and is also better at assessing patients and their needs. He is able to take something from the supervisor and also to reject. The reflection of all the processes in each other means that the supervisor has to change with each supervisee, just as the therapist must change with each patient in order to accommodate the development towards the ability to end.

Leaving the supervisor

Once the trainee becomes a qualified therapist, in some organisations supervision becomes optional. Even if it is expected that therapists continue in supervision after training, there is a case for changing supervisors from time to time in order to avoid falling into ruts and complacency and to learn what others have to teach. How does one broach the need to leave the supervisor? Some make it possible by enquiring each year whether the supervisee wishes to continue for another academic year. Others take continuing for granted and made it extremely difficult for the supervisee to finish. In therapy, there is at least a task which can be said to be completed or as near to complete as it will get. In supervision, there is an ongoing process.

Supervisors who are alert to the difficulty that there might be for the therapist will usually make an ending possible. Supervisees nevertheless enhance a therapist's status and reputation. The work of supervision is a welcome change of pace from therapy itself and it is not surprising that in some cases, a therapist's desire to end or change supervisors might feel like a blow to the narcissism of the supervisor. An extra difficulty arises if the supervisor suspects that the reason for the ending is the supervisor's own incompetence or boredom or a disregard of boundaries. Supervisory relationships can become collegial and very enjoyable. The boundaries need to be maintained but can be more flexible than in therapy, and some supervisors do not maintain a sufficient regard for the need to do the work professionally. The tone of supervision is naturally different from that of therapy, and the supervisor may relax too much and be too expansive about herself. If there is an uneasy awareness that all is not well, then the supervisee's wish to end might well be a criticism.

A supervisor who is growing old or ill or depressed is likely to cease to be useful. Yet a therapist who does not wish to be destructive or to acknowledge destructive impulses will feel anxious about leaving or suggesting an ending. Supervisors in this situation may seem to need their supervisees, and common humanity will make it difficult to say in effect: 'You are too old, or too ill.' Therapists will stay with elderly supervisors to keep them alive, just as patients will stay to heal and repair and keep their therapists going. The supervisor has the responsibility to watch for this and to make sure that an ending is possible when it is needed. In this he is modelling good practice which is essential in all aspects of training and supervision. We have a profession which works at many levels and has theoretical and practical aspects, but above all, training still needs to be a kind of apprenticeship in which supervisors should be master craftsmen, and should try to demonstrate the kind of responsibility and restraint which they demand from their trainees.

Therapists in any of their roles have to be prepared to give up relationships that they have come to enjoy and that they have used for satisfaction, for income and for validation as a worthwhile human being. This is a hard task and is often too difficult. No wonder we need help from each other as colleagues and from present and past teachers and supervisors to bear in mind that the ability to let go when the time comes is one of the primary achievements of any kind of therapy.

References

Clarkson, P. (ed.) (1998) *Supervision*, London: Whurr.

Freeman, T. (1991) 'Hobson's Choice: personal analysis and supervision in the training of psychoanalytic psychotherapists', *British Journal of Psychotherapy* 8 (2): 204.

Macdonald, A. (1992) 'Training and outcome in supervised individual psychotherapy', *British Journal of Psychotherapy* 8 (3): 237.

Stoltenberg, C. and Delworth, U. (1987) *Supervising Counsellors and Therapists*, London: Jossey Bass.

Symington, N. (1986) 'The analyst's act of freedom', in Kohon, G. (ed.) *The Independent Tradition*, London: Free Association Books.

THE GOOD ENDING

All therapists need to envisage ending their own work as therapists and supervisors. We all need to make a therapeutic will which will allow for the safe care of our patients and supervisees in the event of an accident or sudden death. Even more difficult for many is to plan retirement and put it into practice. Like our patients, we also need to be able to let it all go and say that we have done enough before that recognition is enforced by illness or debility or incompetence. Working in the field of psychotherapy is one of the most fascinating and rewarding experiences that anyone can have. Yet we all come to the end of a useful working life sooner or later and can learn to exist without patients to help us. It is therefore essential some day to be able to choose to say that I have done my share, had my turn and now I shall leave it to others.

INDEX

loss 2, 4, 14, 17–18, 31, 37–8, 41–2, 46, 56, 78, 95, 131, 139–41, 143, 146–7, 149–50, 156, 164

Macdonald, A. 3, 163, 165
Mahler, M. 40, 54
Malan, D. 151
Mann, J. 156
meconnaissance 140
Melzer, D. 18, 52–4
memory: as cause 12, 28, 135–6; generation of 29; recovery of 13, 24, 32, 38, 92, 120; redescription process 31
Mill, J. 102–3
Miller, I. 37–8
Mohammed, C. and Smith, R. 151
Molino, A. 140
Mollon, P. 47, 75
Molnos, A. 136, 152
Murdin, L. *see Clarkson, P.*

nachtraglichkeit 30
narcissism 44–60; and religion 50; therapist's 6, 28, 30, 45, 121, 169–70
negative therapeutic reaction 143
Nemiah, J. 73
normal symbiosis 54

obsessions 73–4, 107
Oedipus complex 18, 19, 26, 30, 34, 36, 73, 83, 153–4
omnipotence: therapist's 19; patient's 38, 55; and narcissism 47–8, 50–1; relinquishment 62, 113–15
Orlinsky, D. *see Howard, K.*
outcome 3, 6, 12, 15, 20, 28, 44, 99, 103, 129, 151, 157–8, 163, 165

paranoid schizoid position 8, 17–18
paraphrenics 52
Parens, H. *see Akhtar, S.*
Parkes, C 139

Philips, A. 31, 65
projection 17–18, 44, 55, 108, 162
psychosis 30, 38, 119

Ragland, E 63
referral 65, 82, 88, 91, 93, 100, 111, 119, 129, 150
regression 82, 87–9, 151, 154
repetition compulsion 28, 63–4, 70, 73, 120
repression 15, 30–4, 104
resistance 5, 16–7, 33, 36–8, 55, 149, 151–2, 165, 167
Rickmann, J. 20
Rowan, J. 154–5

Samuels, A. 13, 66–7
Sandler, J., Dare, C. and Holder, A. 143
Schachter, J. 80
Searles, H 19, 30, 89
self-concept 81
self object 18, 54, 81–3
sexuality 18, 67–8, 73, 94, 111–12
Shapiro, D. 150
Smith, R. *see Mohammed, C.*
Spence, D. 16
Steiner, J. 18
Stern, D. 54
Stoltenberg, C. and Delworth, U. 169
subjectivity 29, 33, 109, 121
suggestion 10, 16
suicide 8–9, 38, 112–15, 127–30
Sundelson, J. *see Bollas, C.*
supervision 2, 9, 91, 95, 125, 129, 160–71
symbolic 41–50, 55, 87
Symington, N. 54, 71, 166
symptoms 2, 12, 14–16, 20, 30, 33, 74, 94, 143, 155

time limited therapy 20, 118, 149–56; short term therapy 10
training 2, 70, 142, 150; analysis for 56–7; ending therapy in 160–71

transference 23, 29, 32–41, 63, 70, 99, 112, 146, 153, 161–2; acting in 28 ; boundaries in 117; encouragement of 122, 157; ethics of 120–2; love 25; maternal 89; resolution of 35; *see also deprivation*

unconscious 6, 14–16, 29, 31, 33, 37, 41, 61, 63, 68, 97–8, 106
United Kingdom Council for Psychotherapy 118, 131

values 2, 10, 38, 97–106, 111–5, 127
Voltaire 59

Westminster Pastoral Foundation 151
will: therapeutic 82, 172
Winnicott, D. 1986 40, 54, 65, 143, 155, 141; 1985 87, 68

Zysman, S. *see Klimovsky, G.*